# This coloring book belongs to:

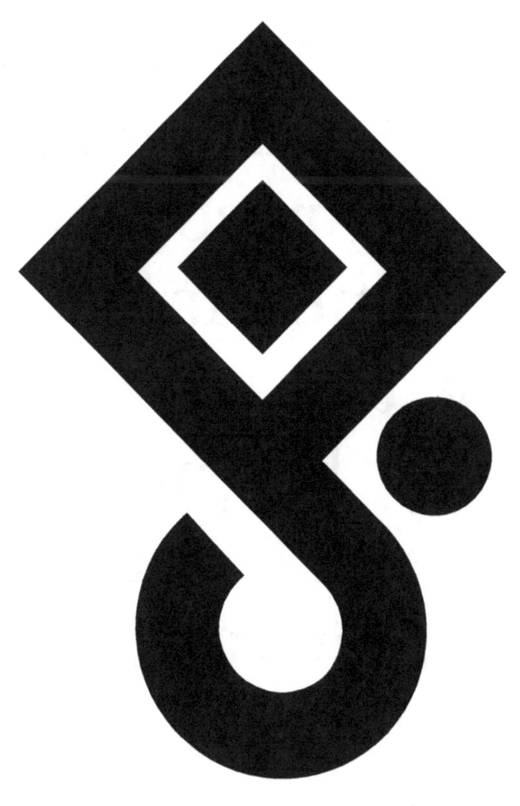

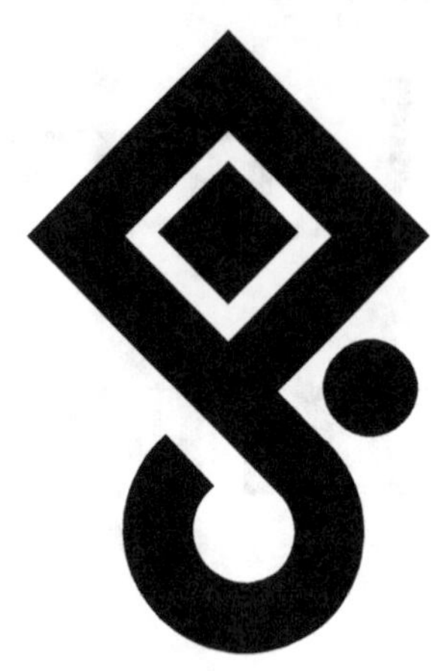

*Thank you for the support!*
*Happy coloring!*

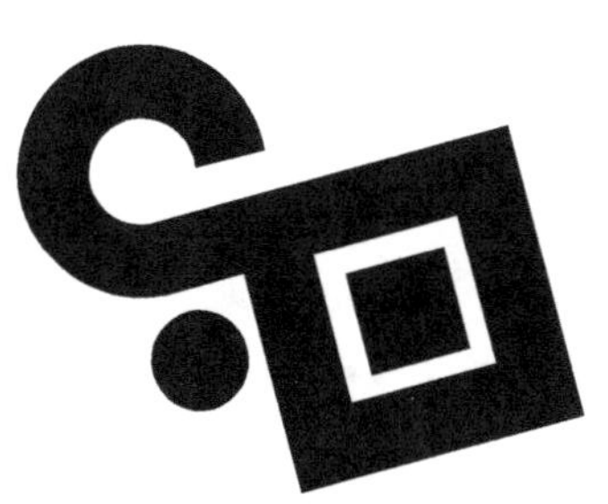

*Share on Instagram with **#colorells** and show off your coloring masterpiece.*

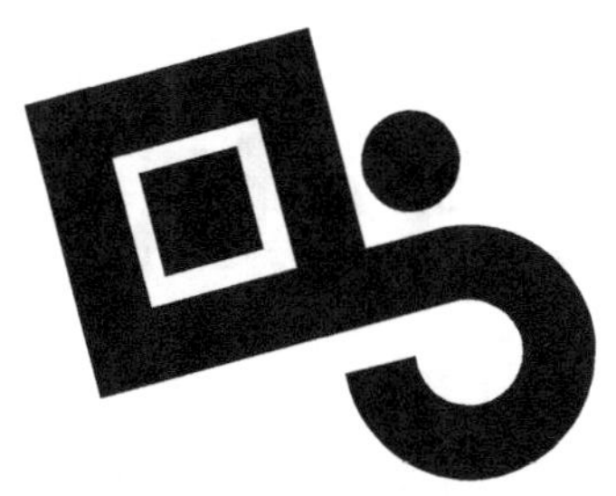

***The Odd Sort - Adult coloring book***

***By Russell McCants***

The lady with the floating head!

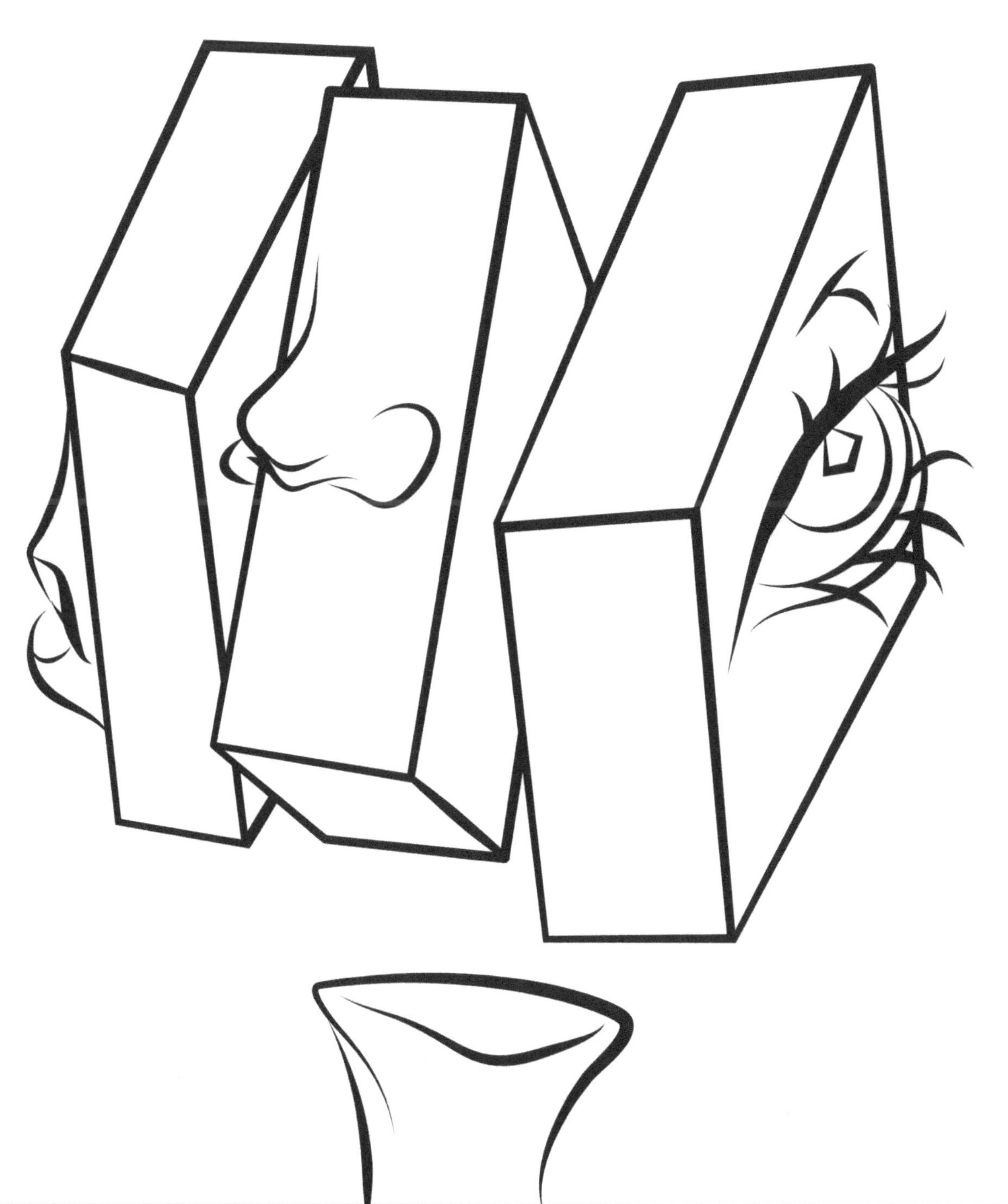

# Meet Rubic

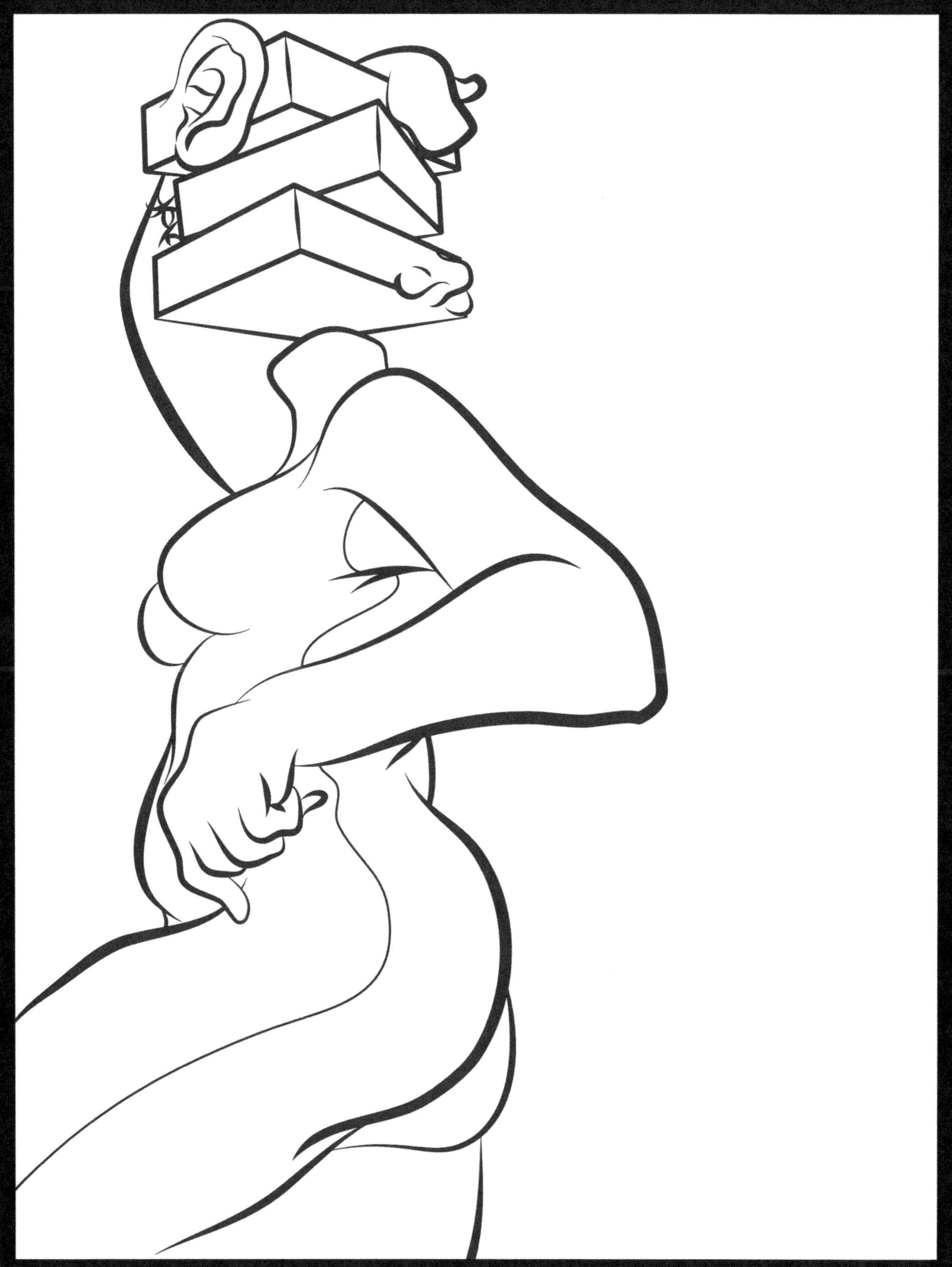

Marvelous...

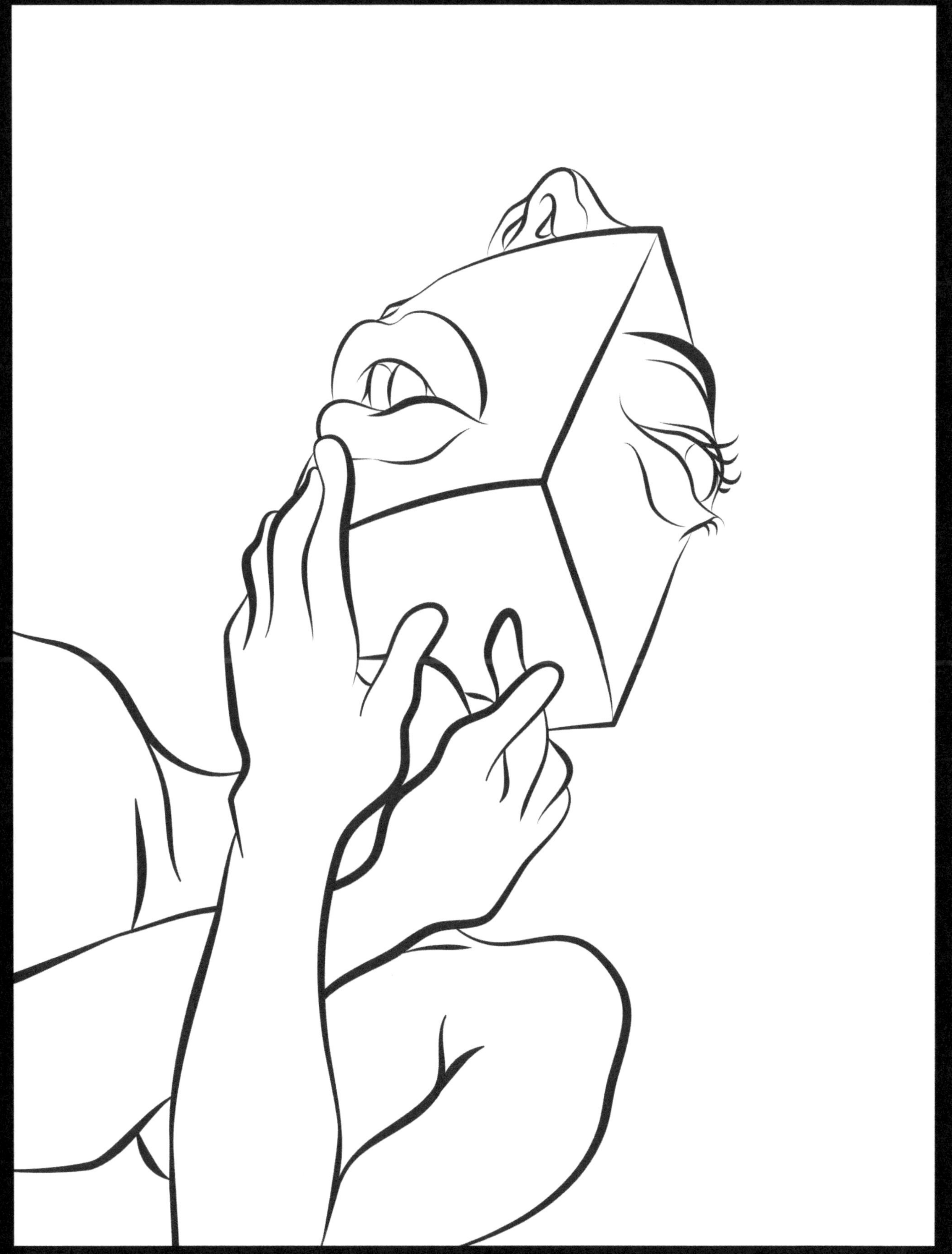

Yet strange.

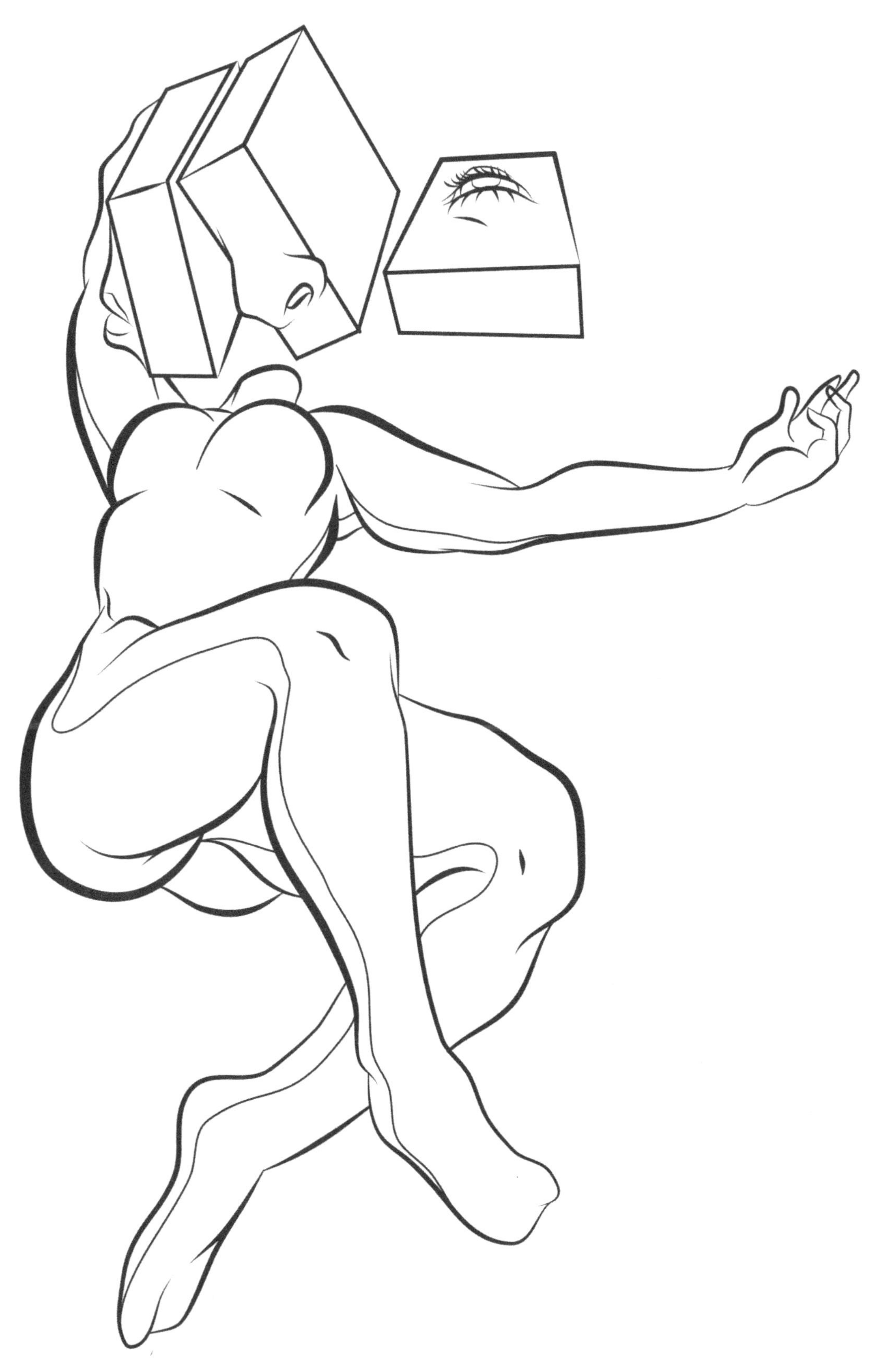

The strongest man known to mankind!

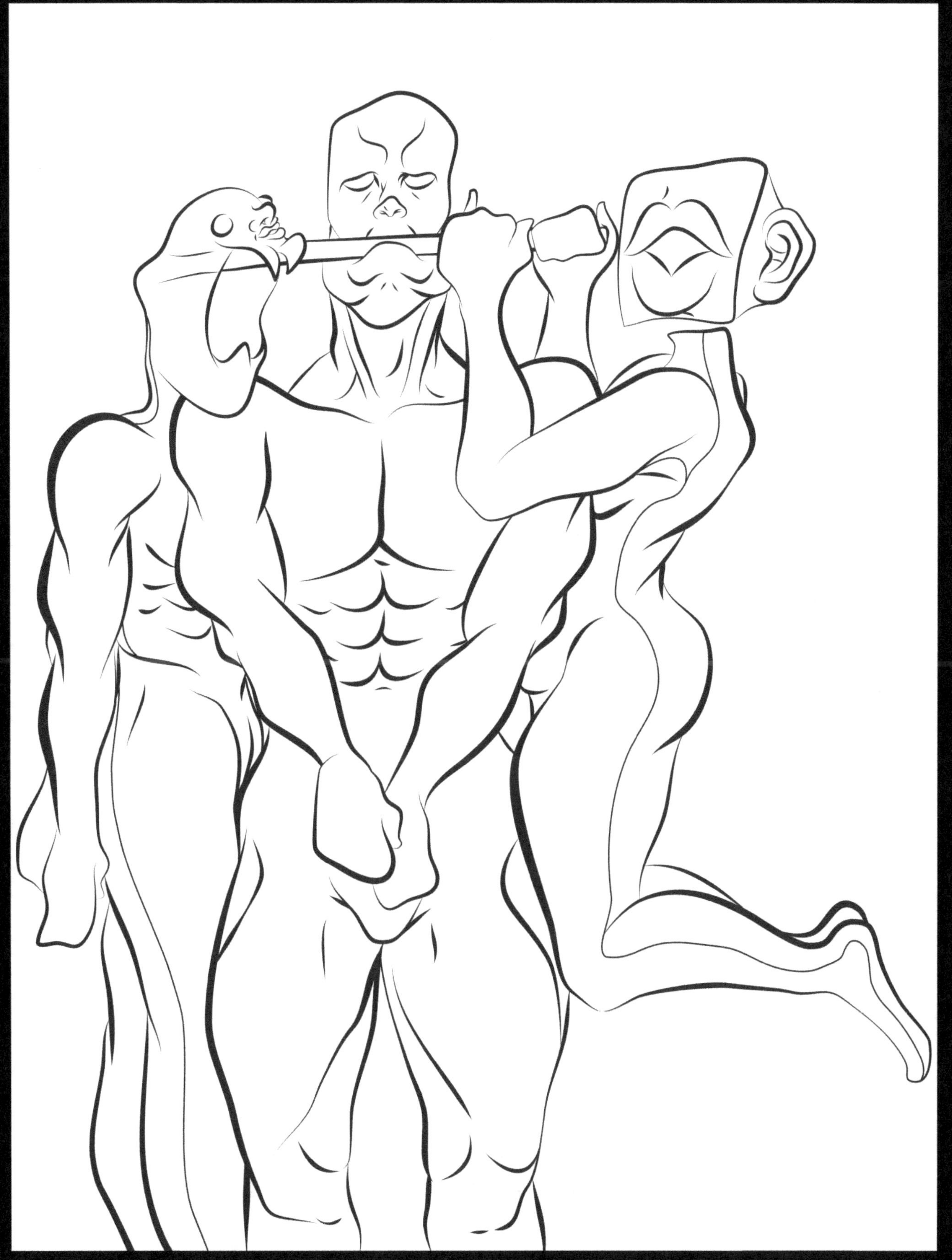

# Meet Coy

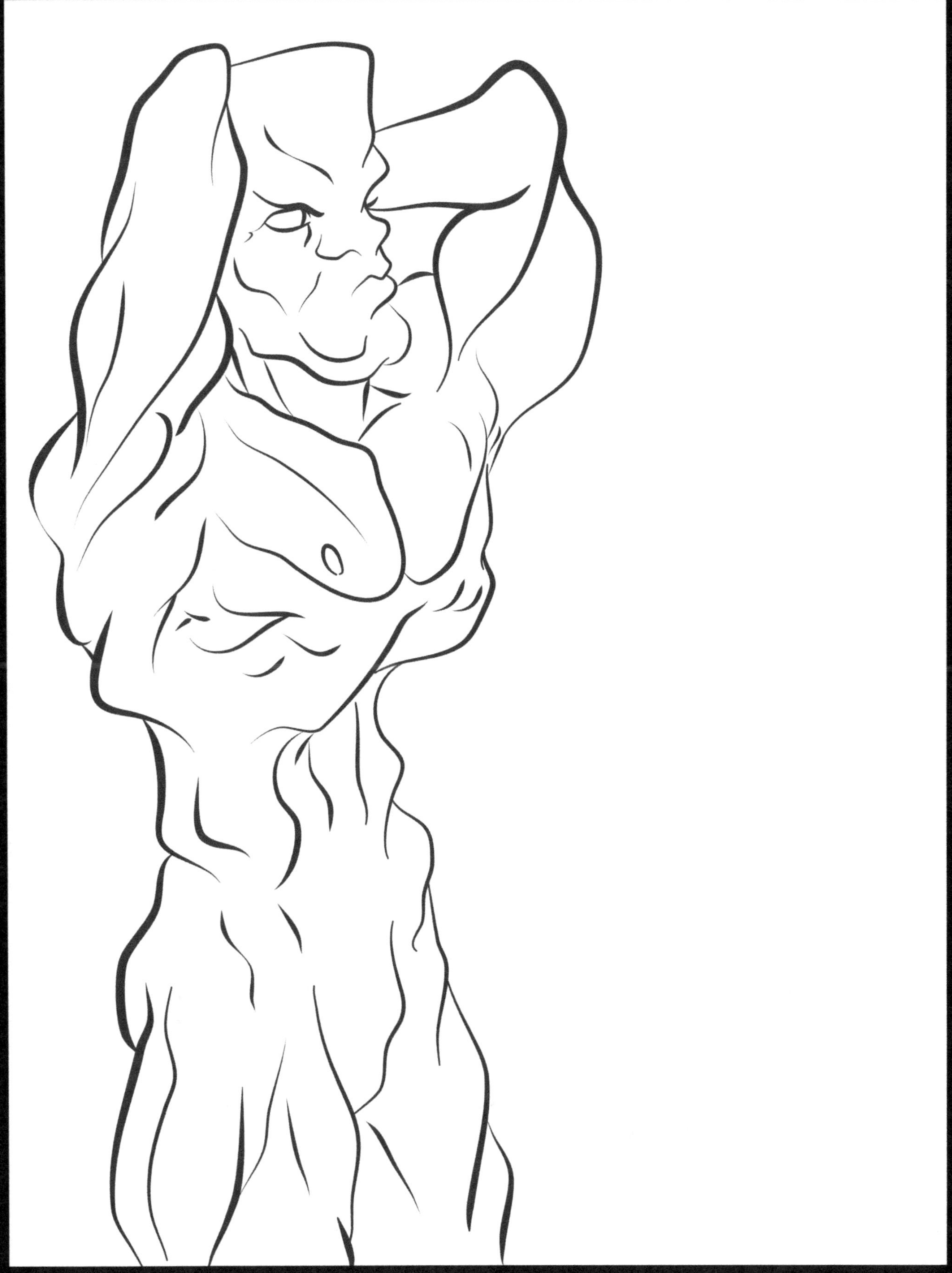

His physique
may entice.

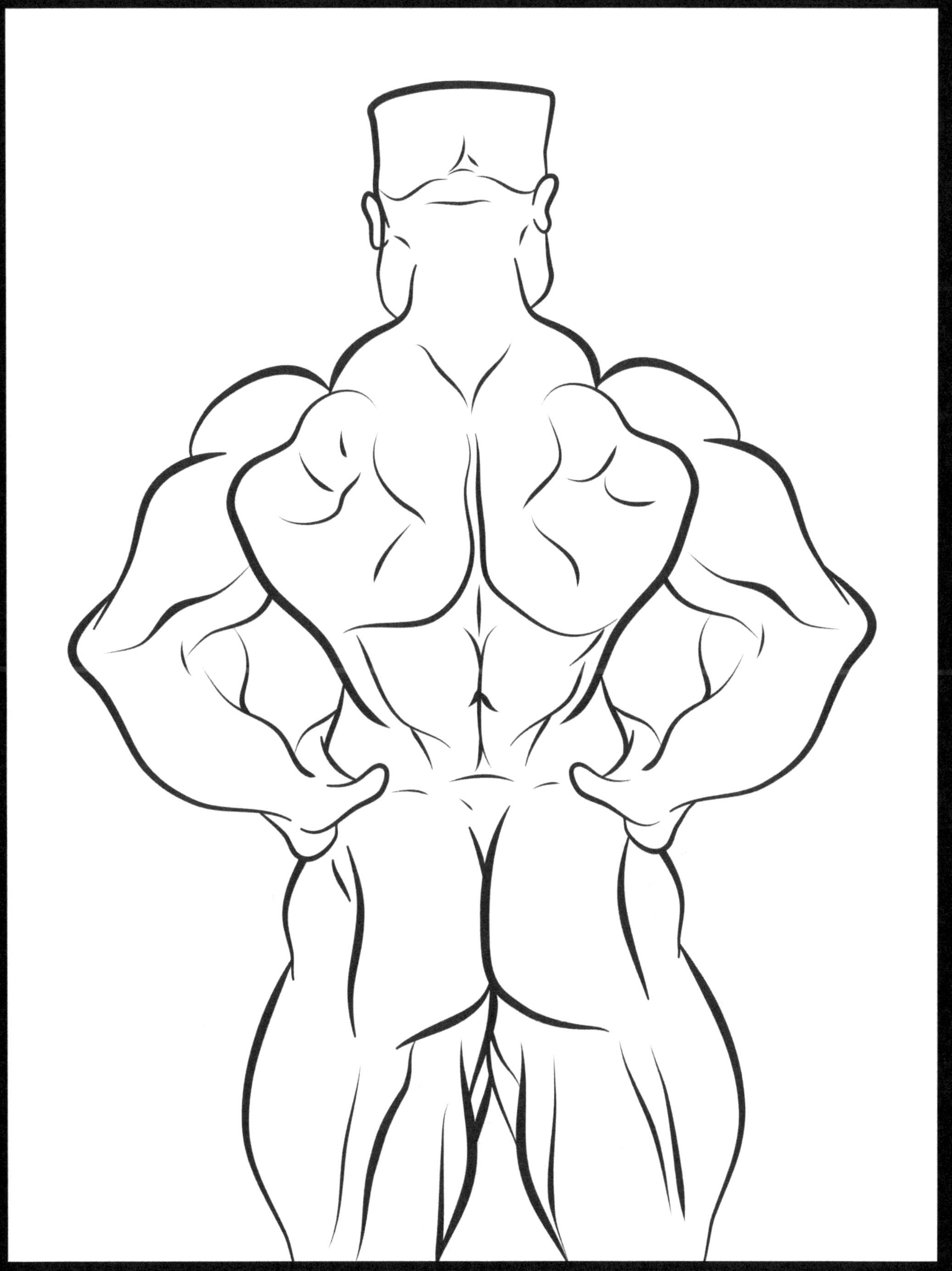

The ever elusive cutout wonder!

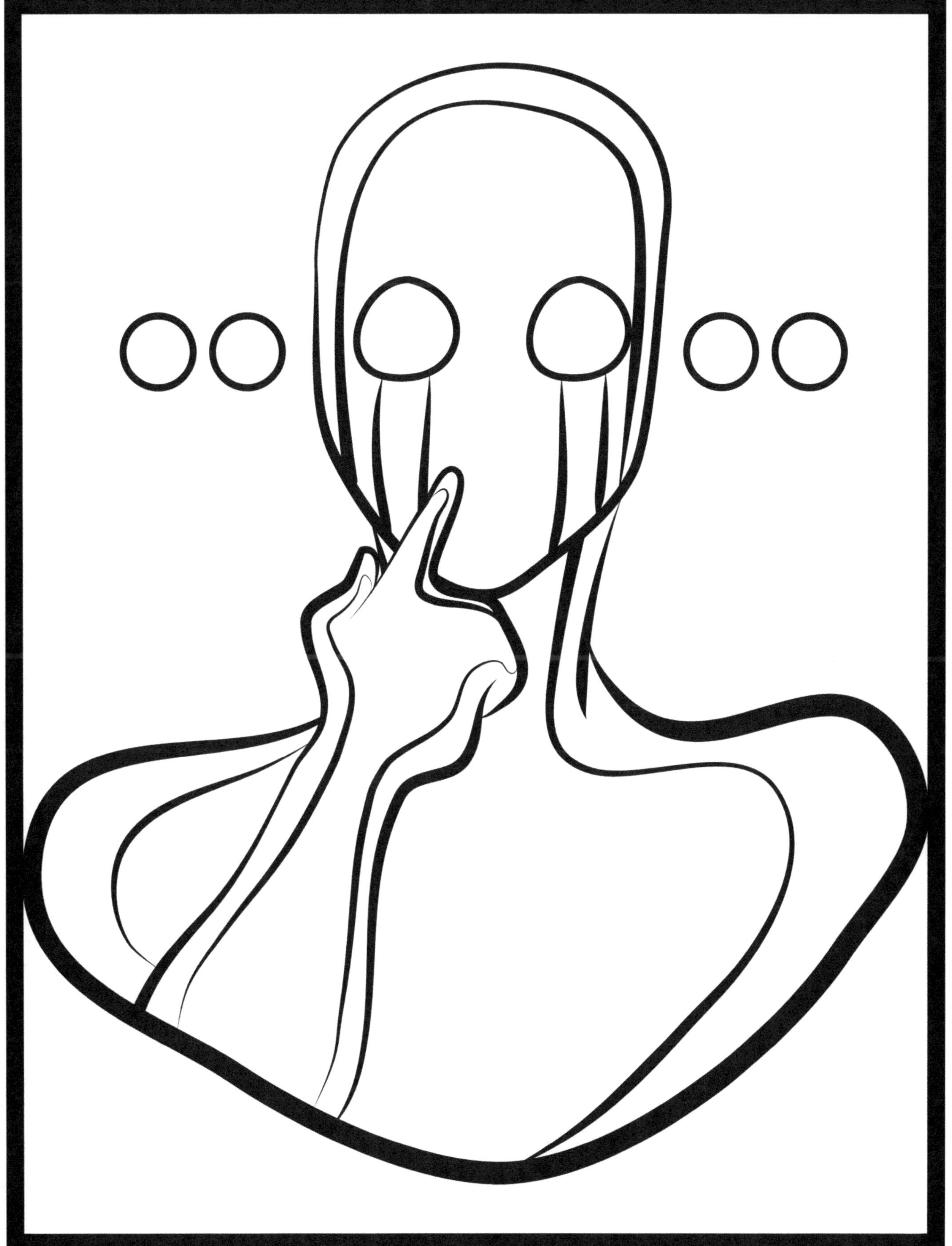

# Meet Crease

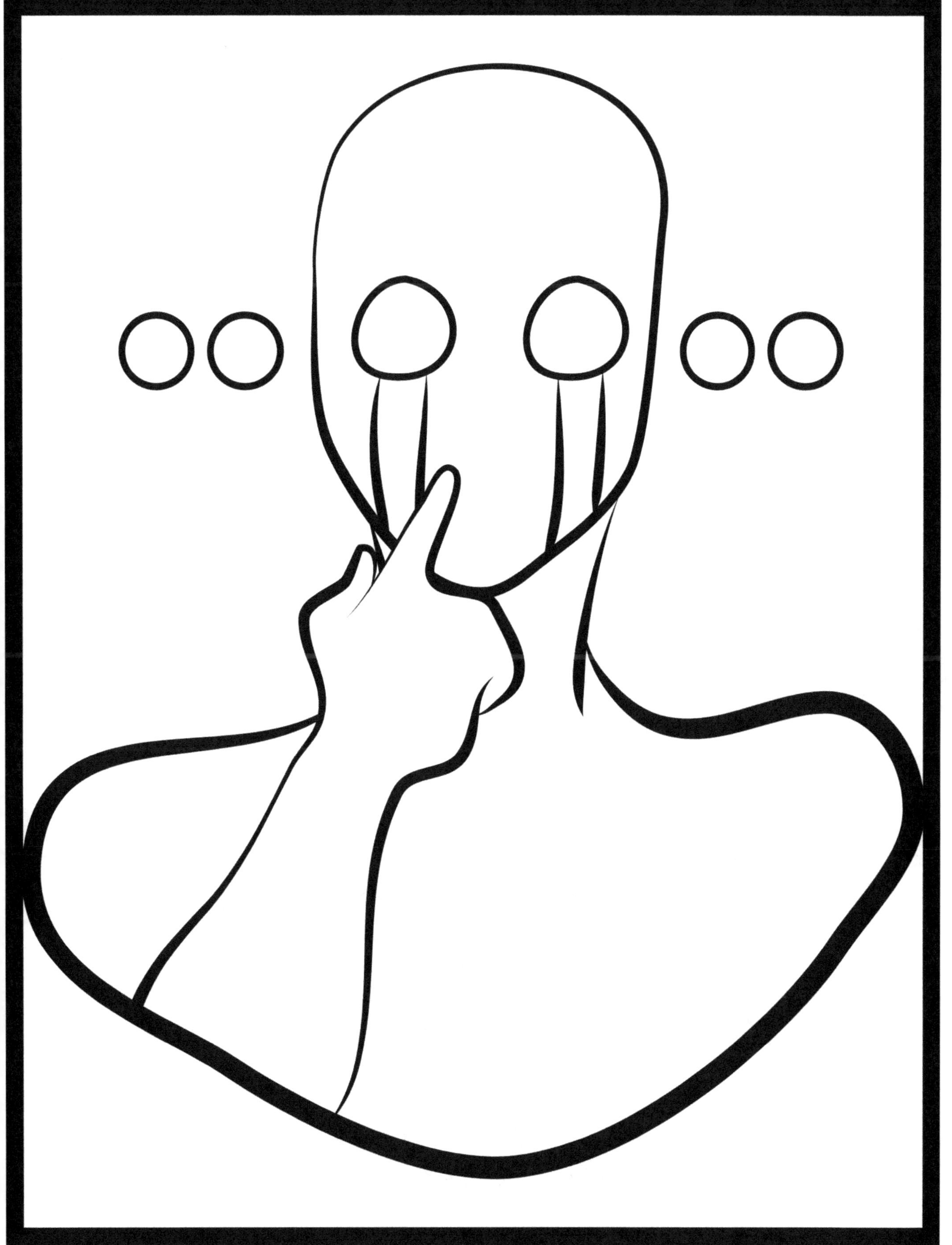

He may need some pointers on that stretch.

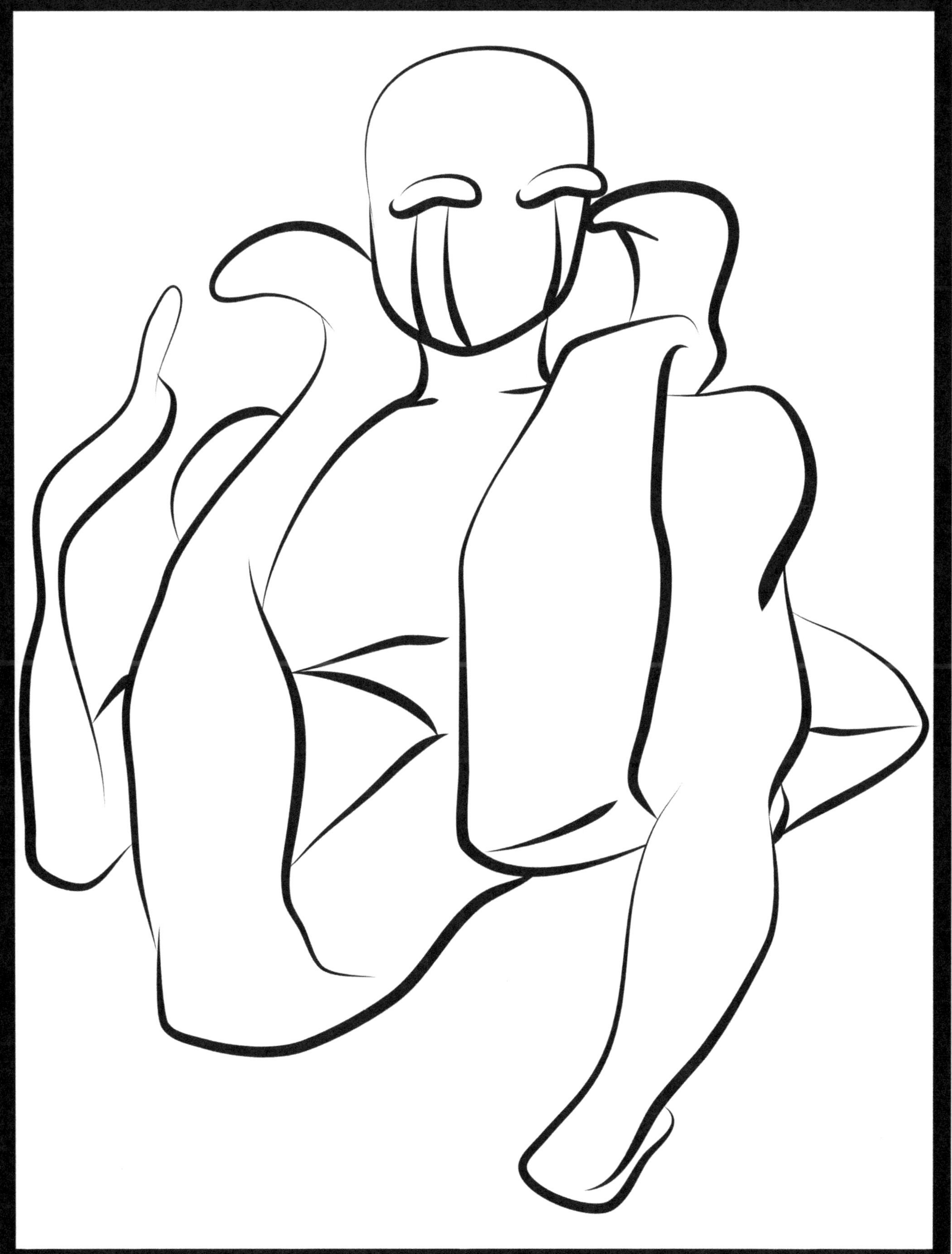

Want your fortune told?!

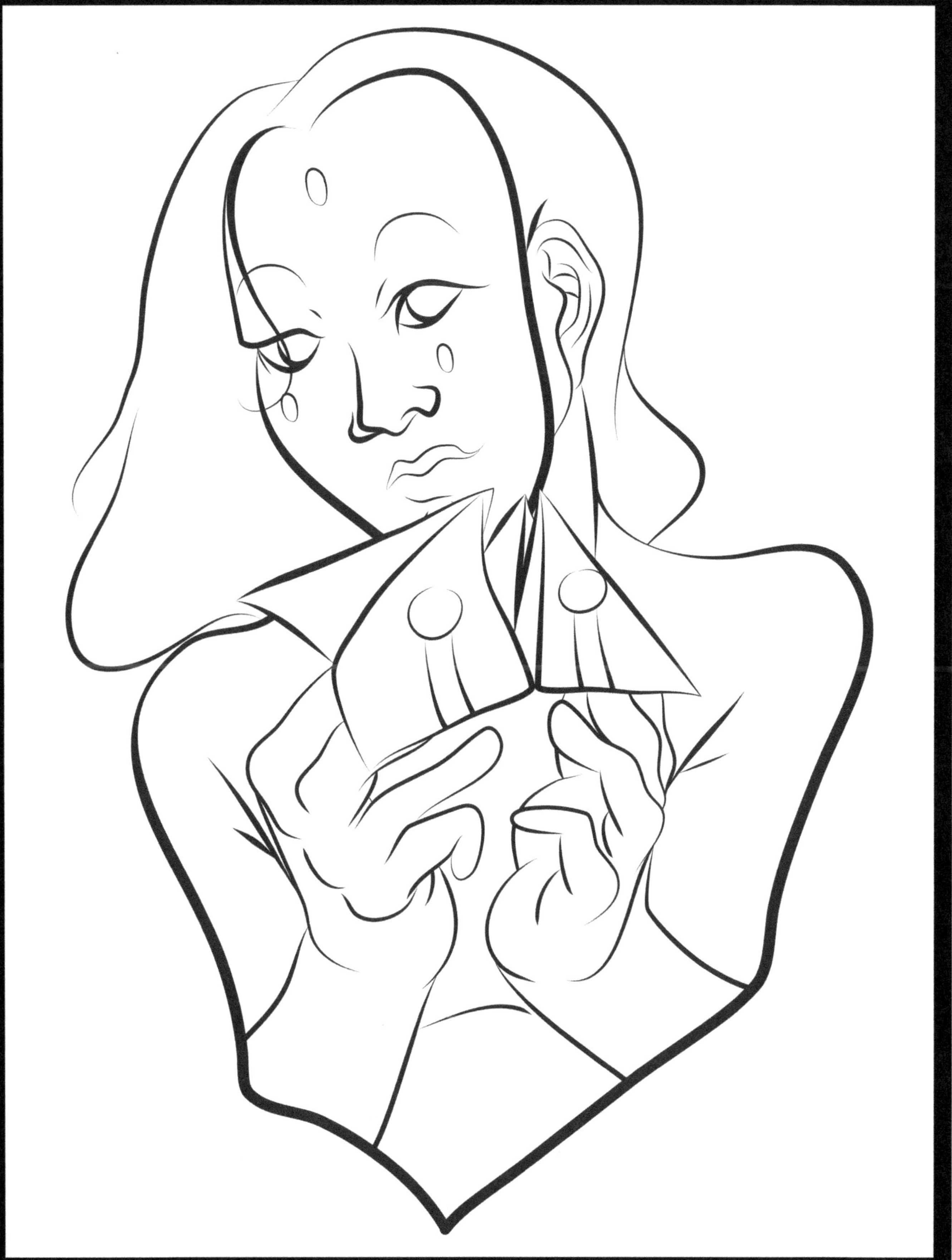

# Meet Dot

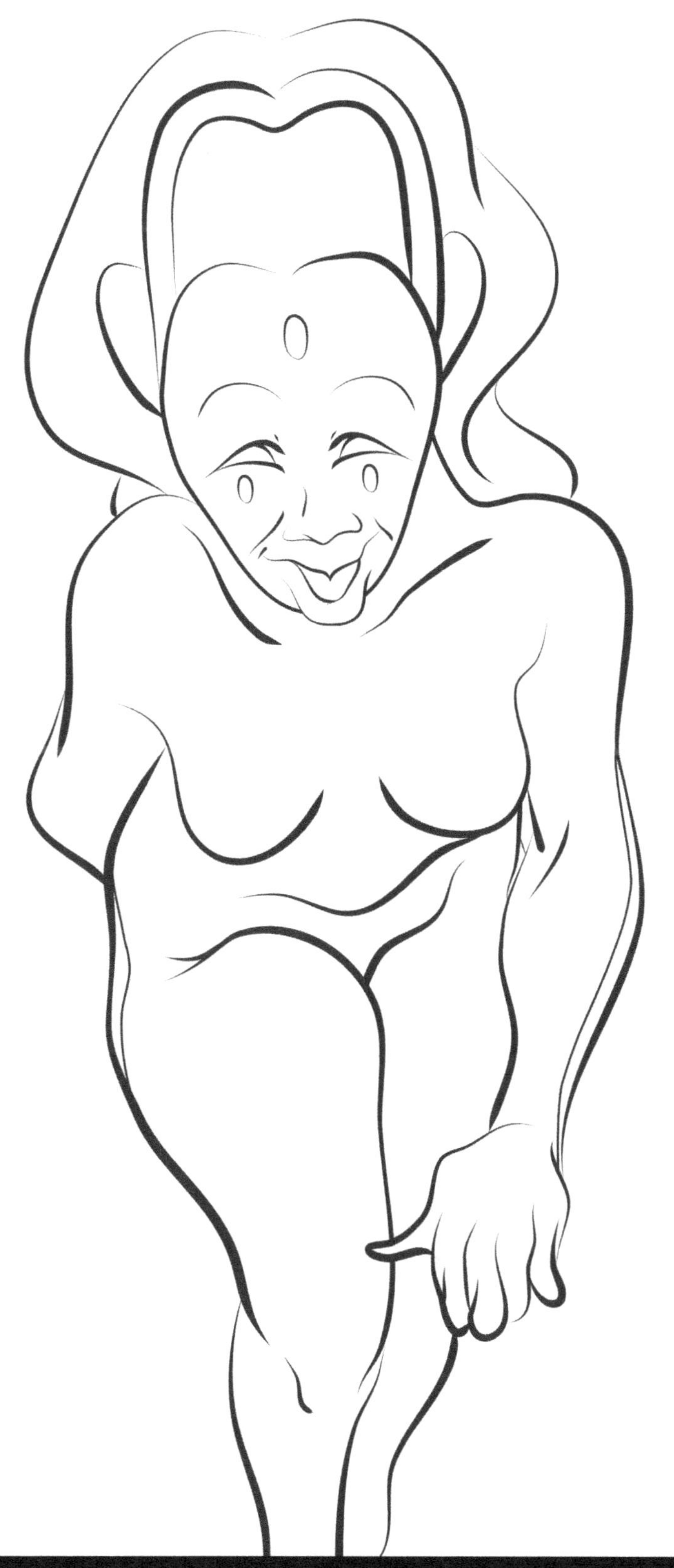

Seems to be an interesting card she picked, but what does it mean?

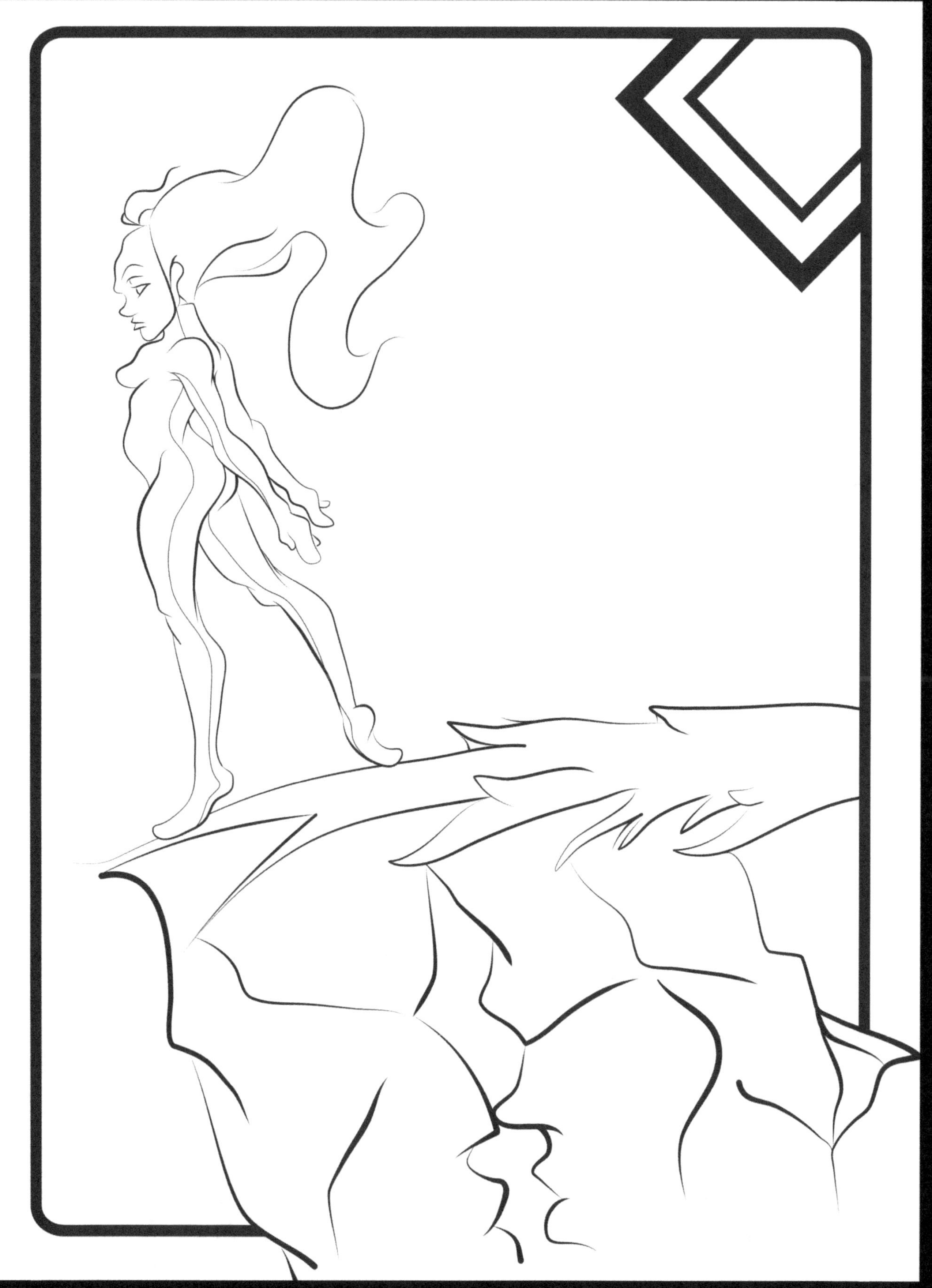

Next is our newest addition to the family!

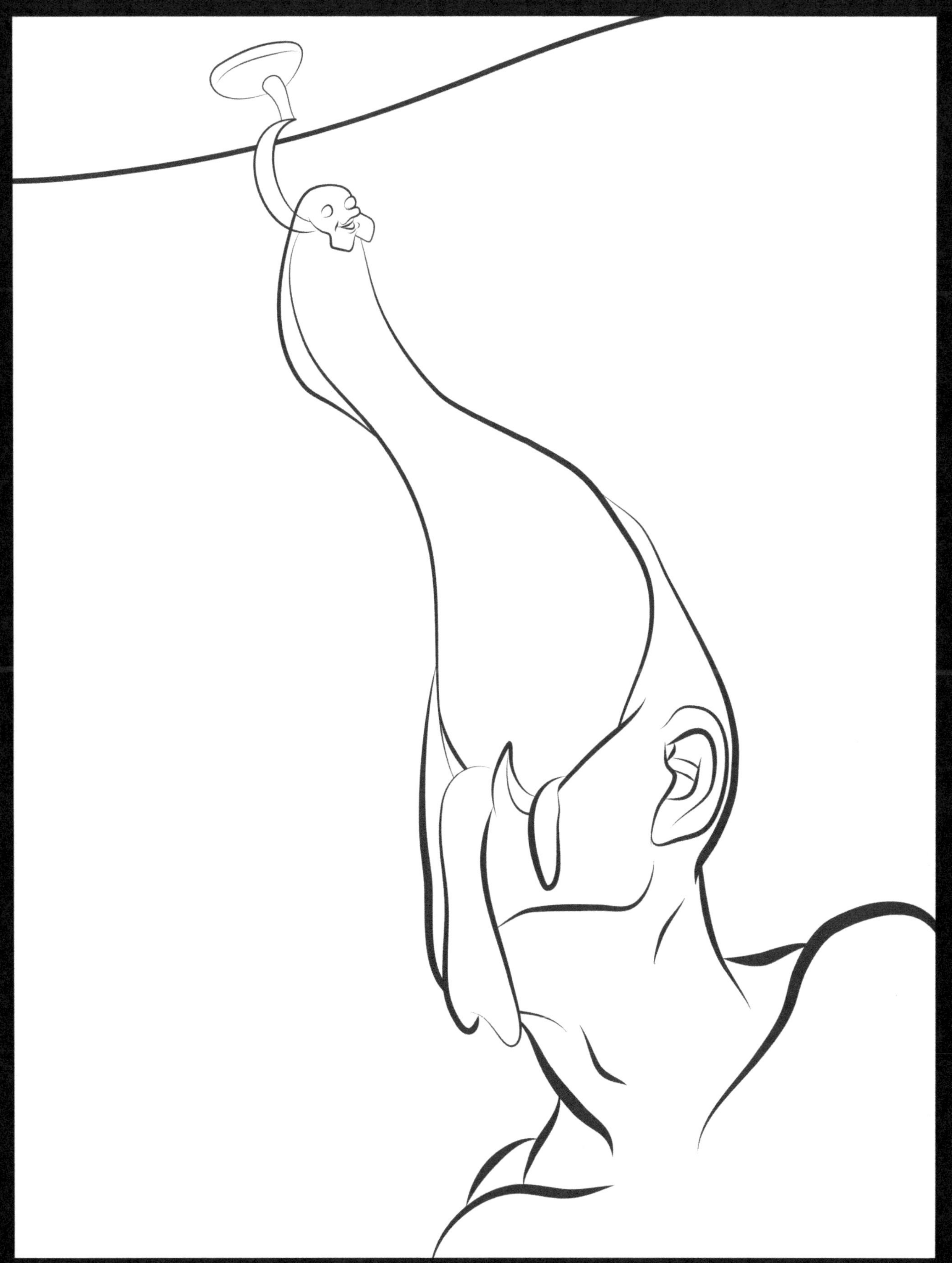

# Meet Eldritch

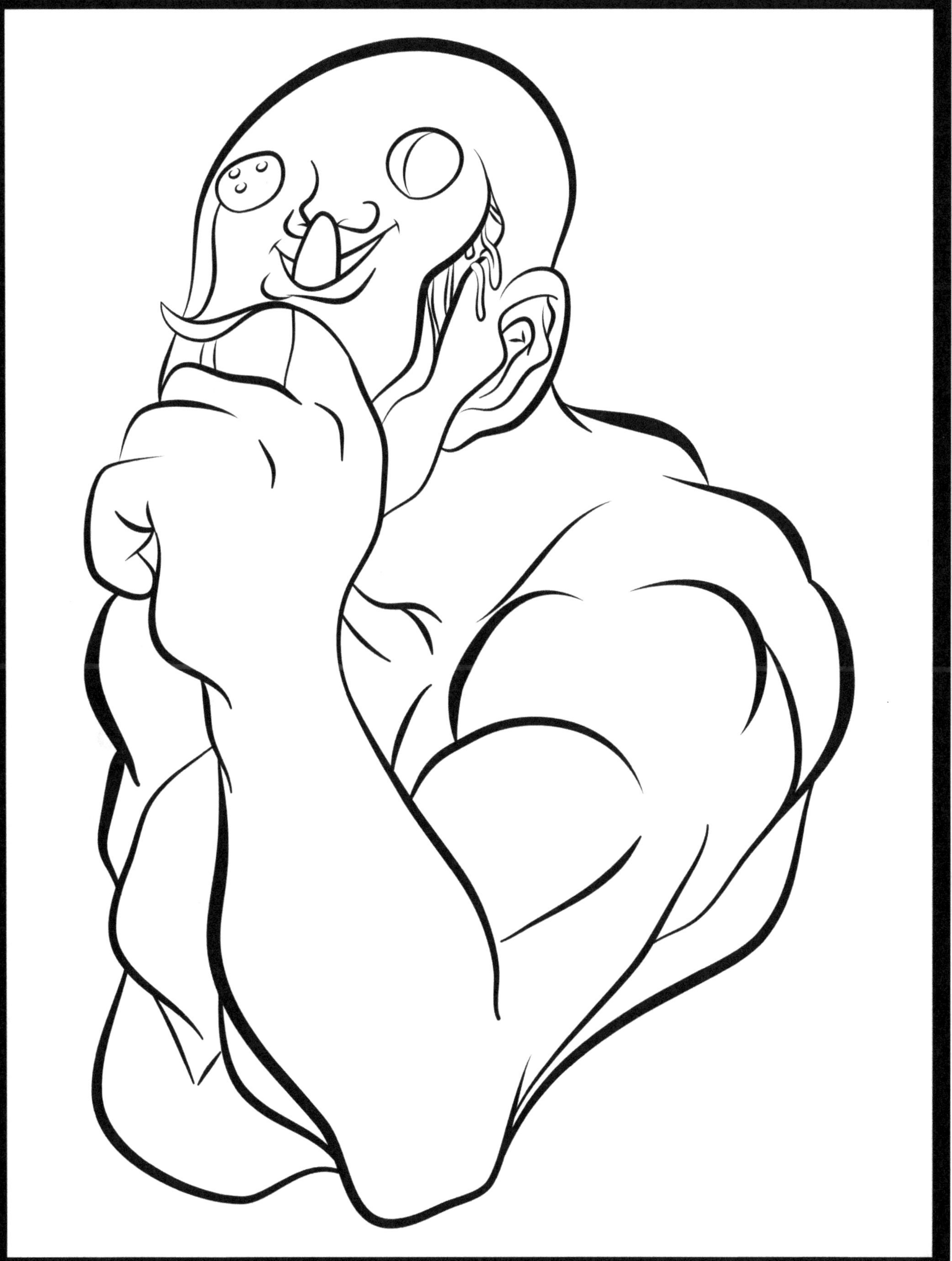

He's dying to
entertain!

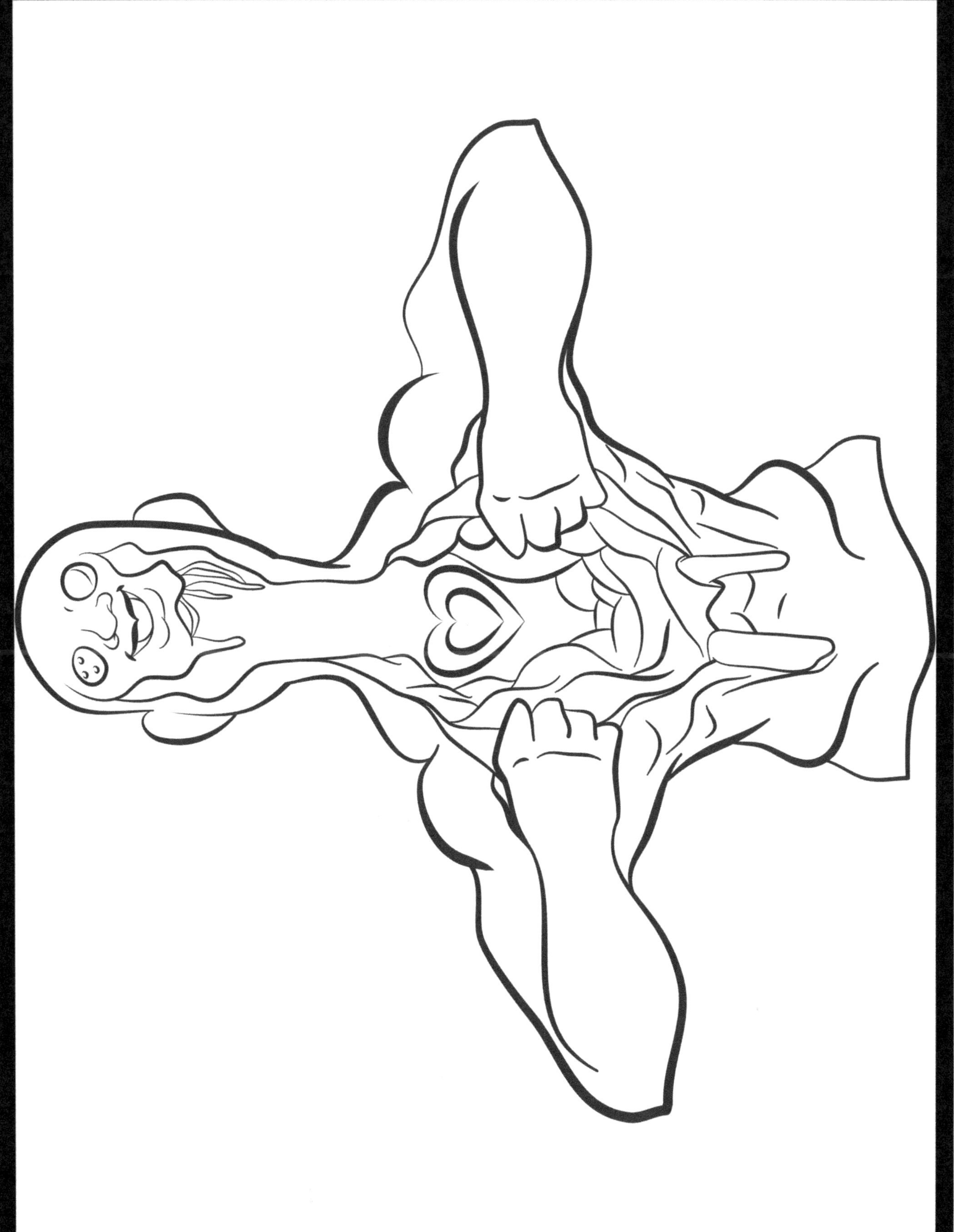

Ah, time for everyone's favorite little gremlin!

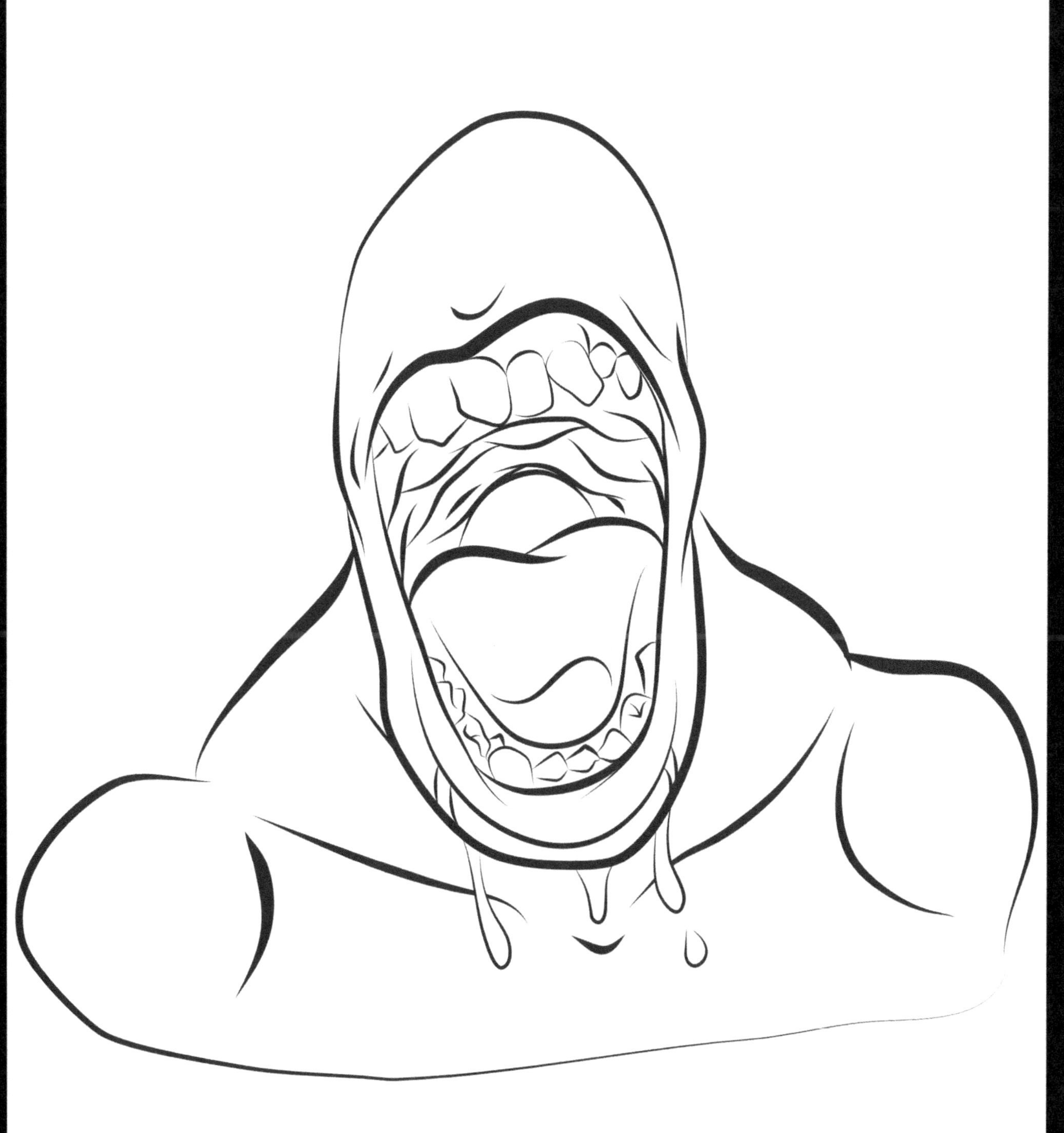

# Meet Mouthy

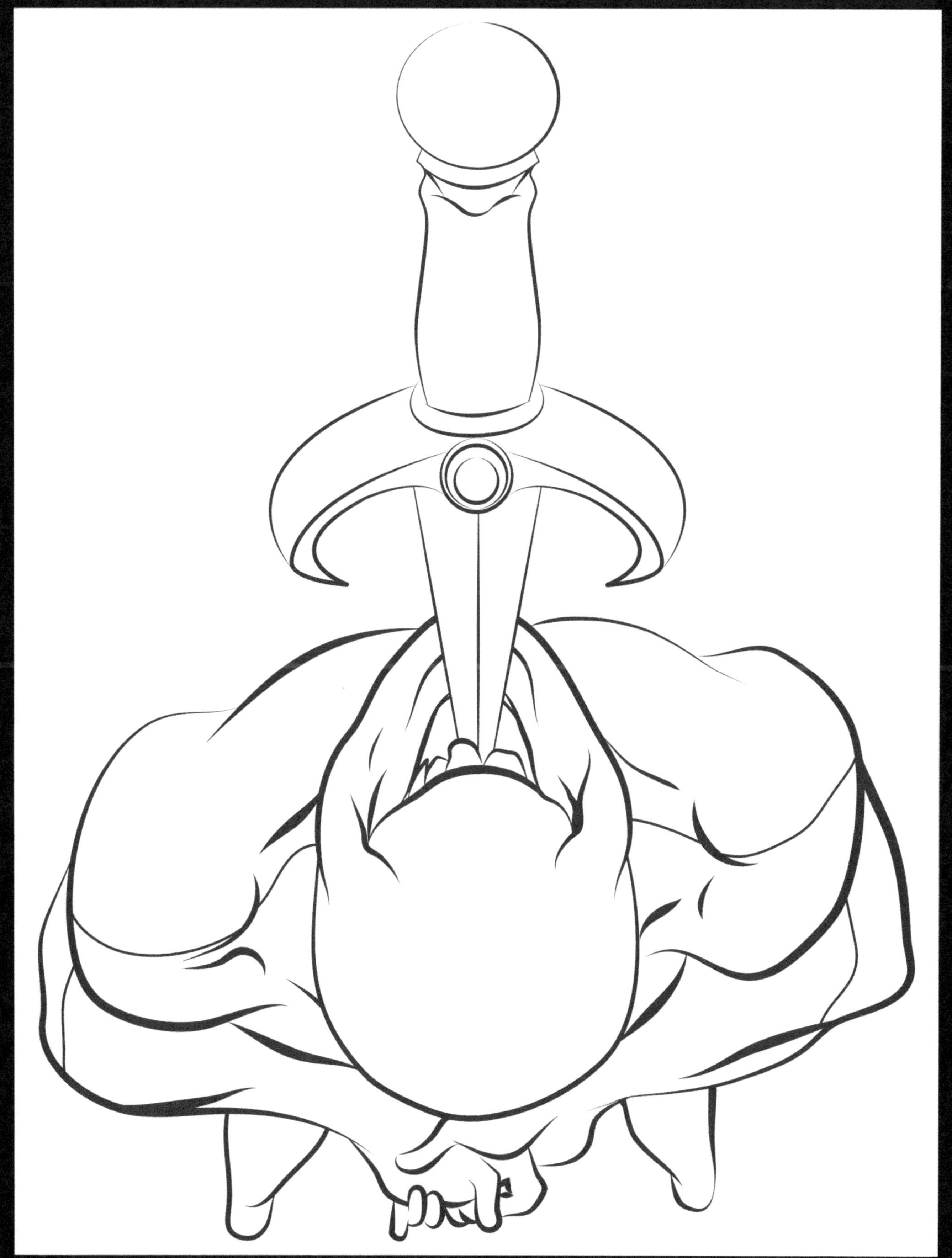

Quite
mischievous
that one.

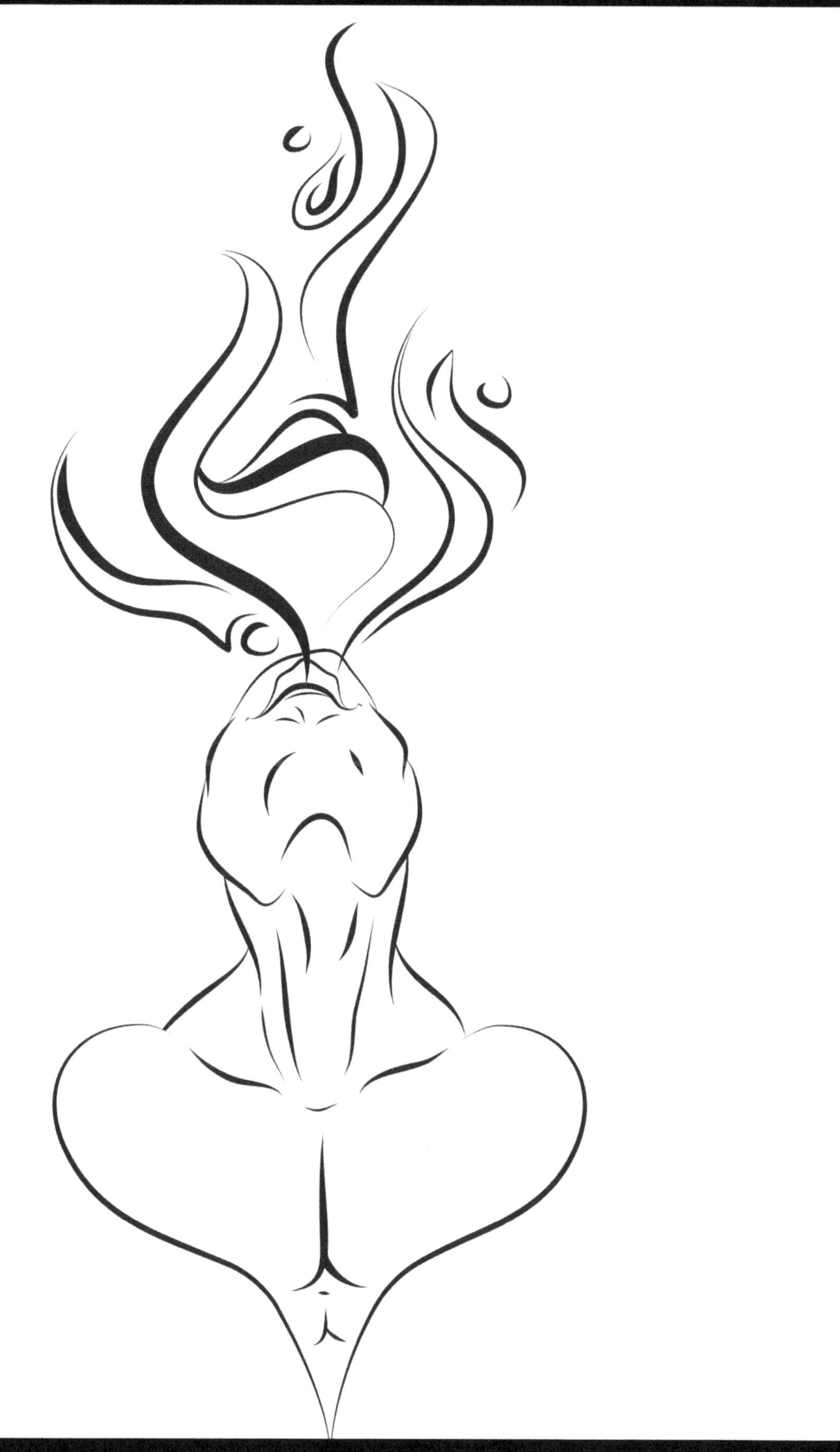

Try drawing a pattern.

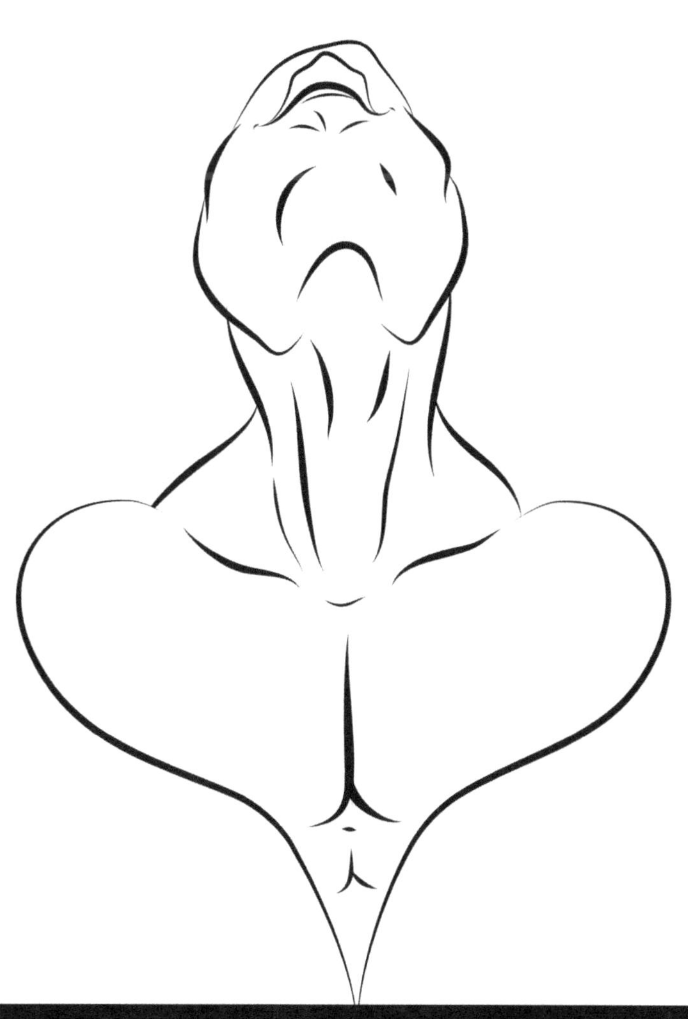

Here’s a crowd pleaser!

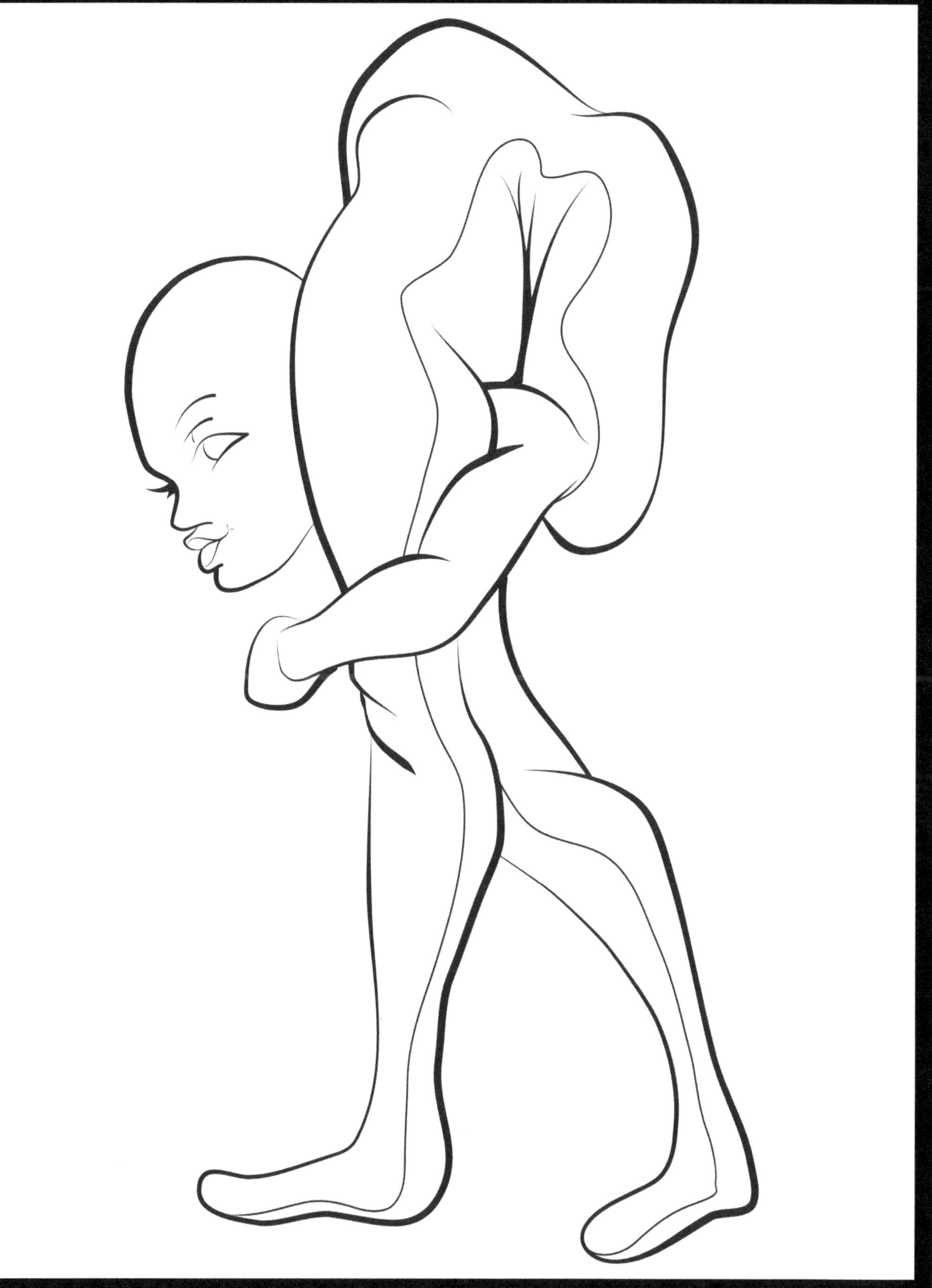

# Meet Pretzel

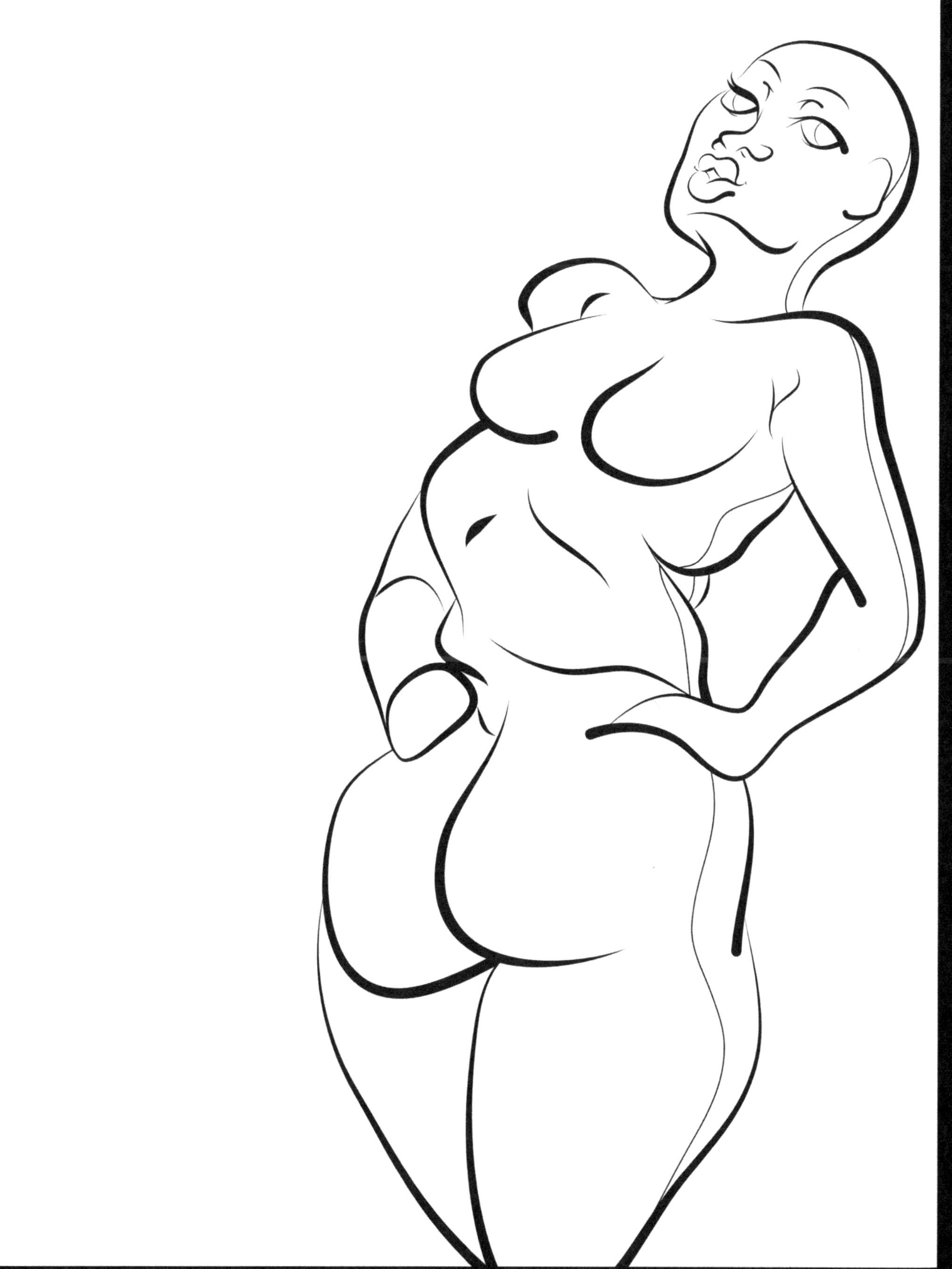

Always
mesmerizing...

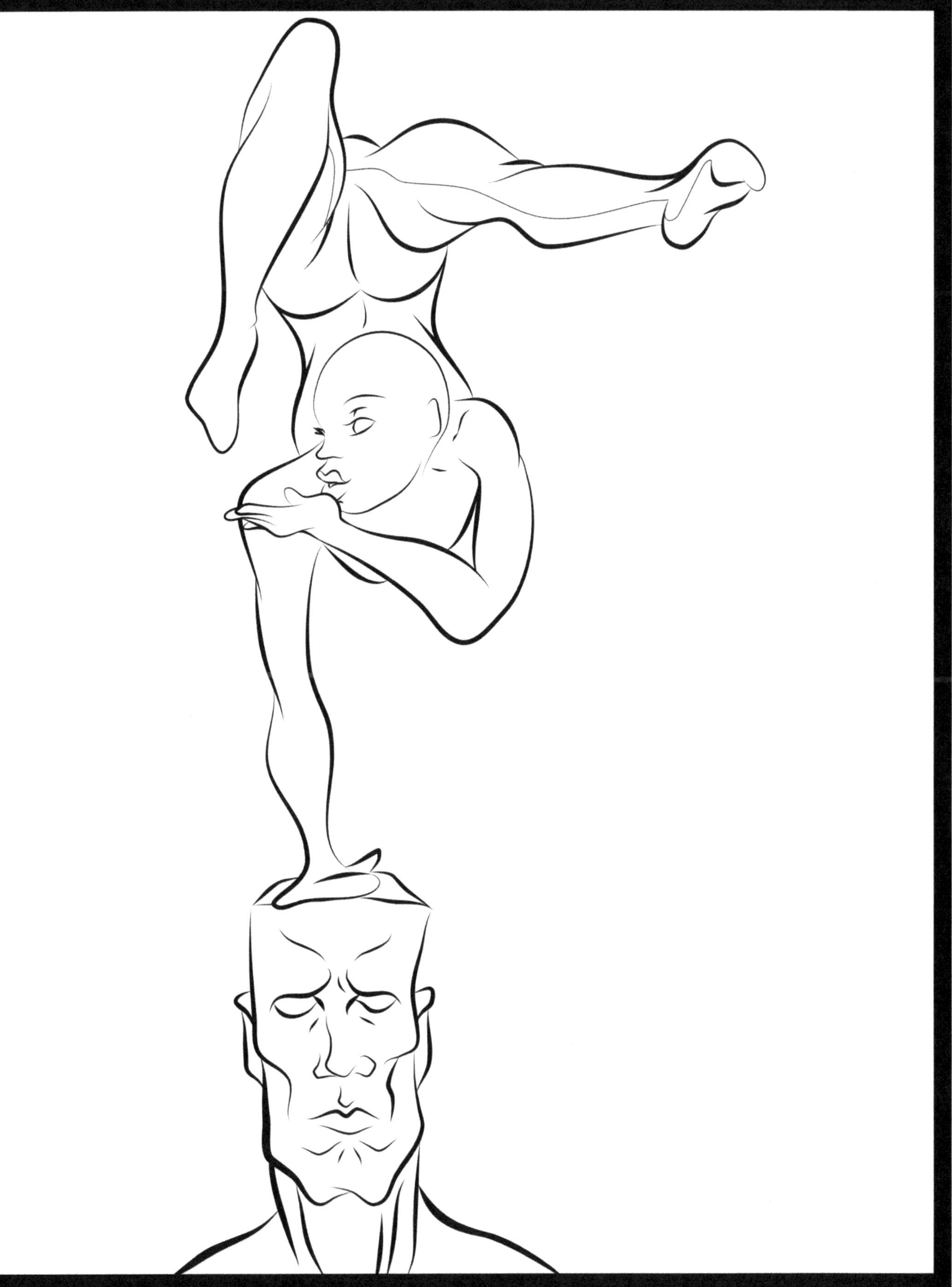

Yet always a bit frightening.

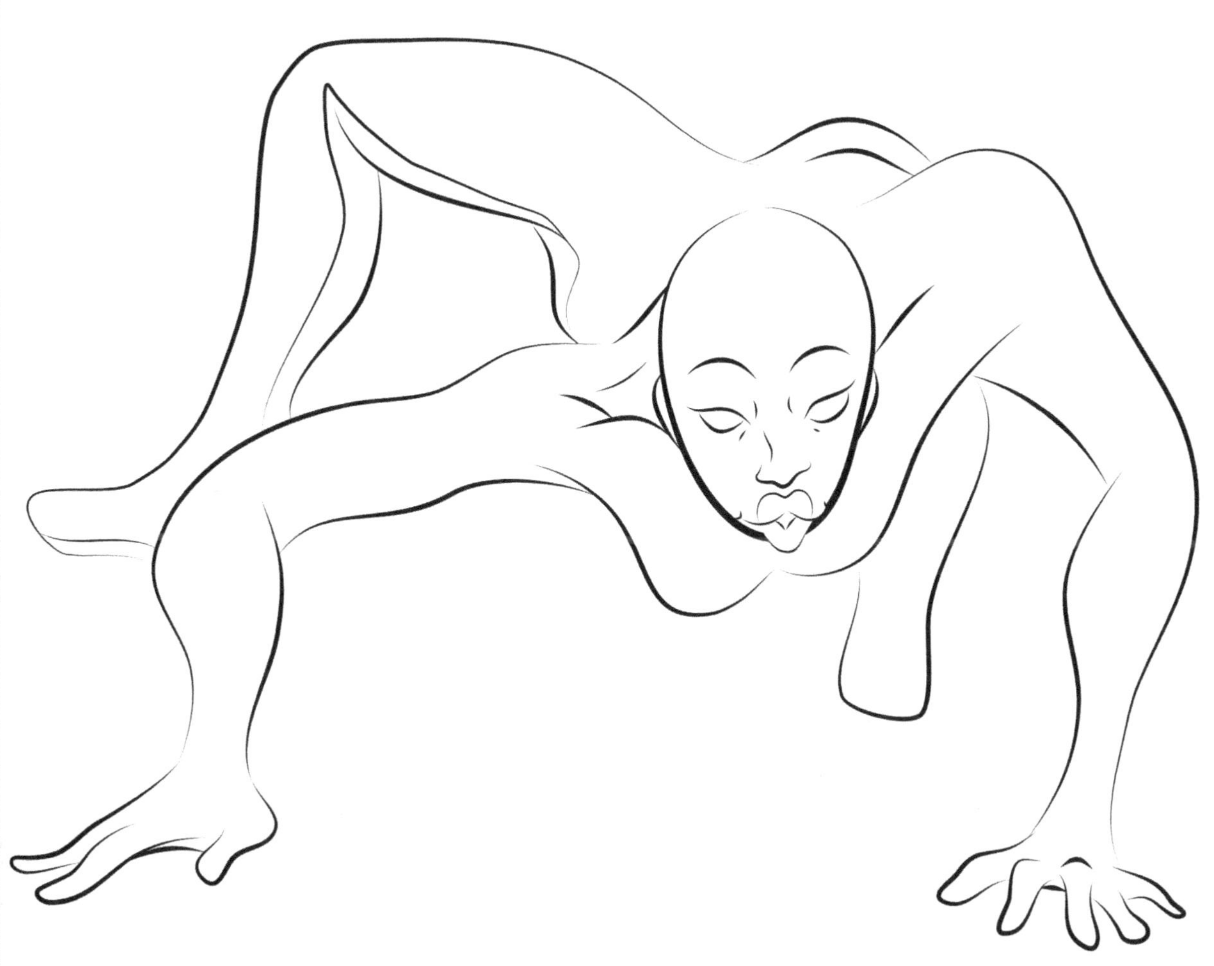

Might I say that's a handsome devil.

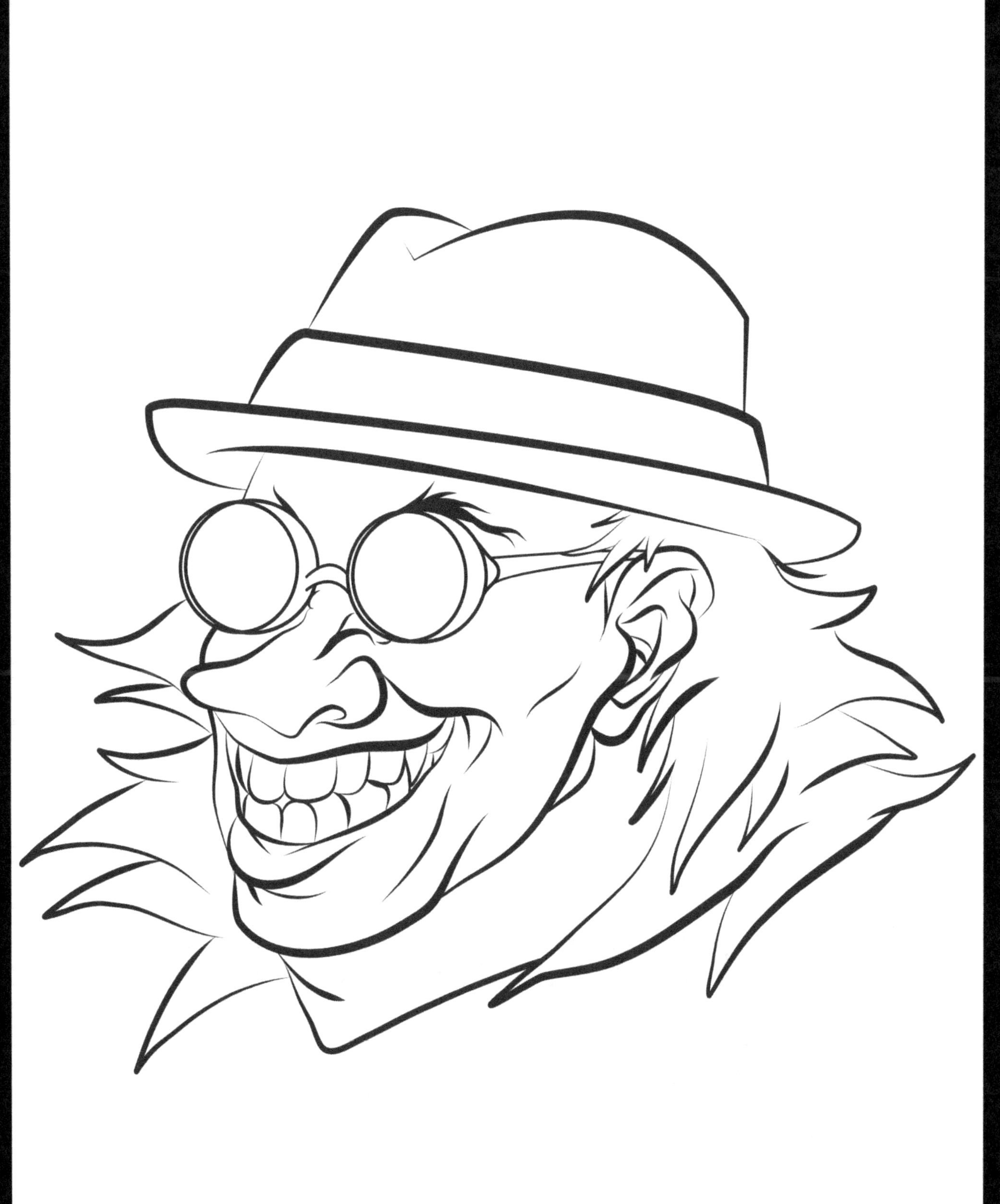

Its rare to catch a glimpse of the Ringmaster.

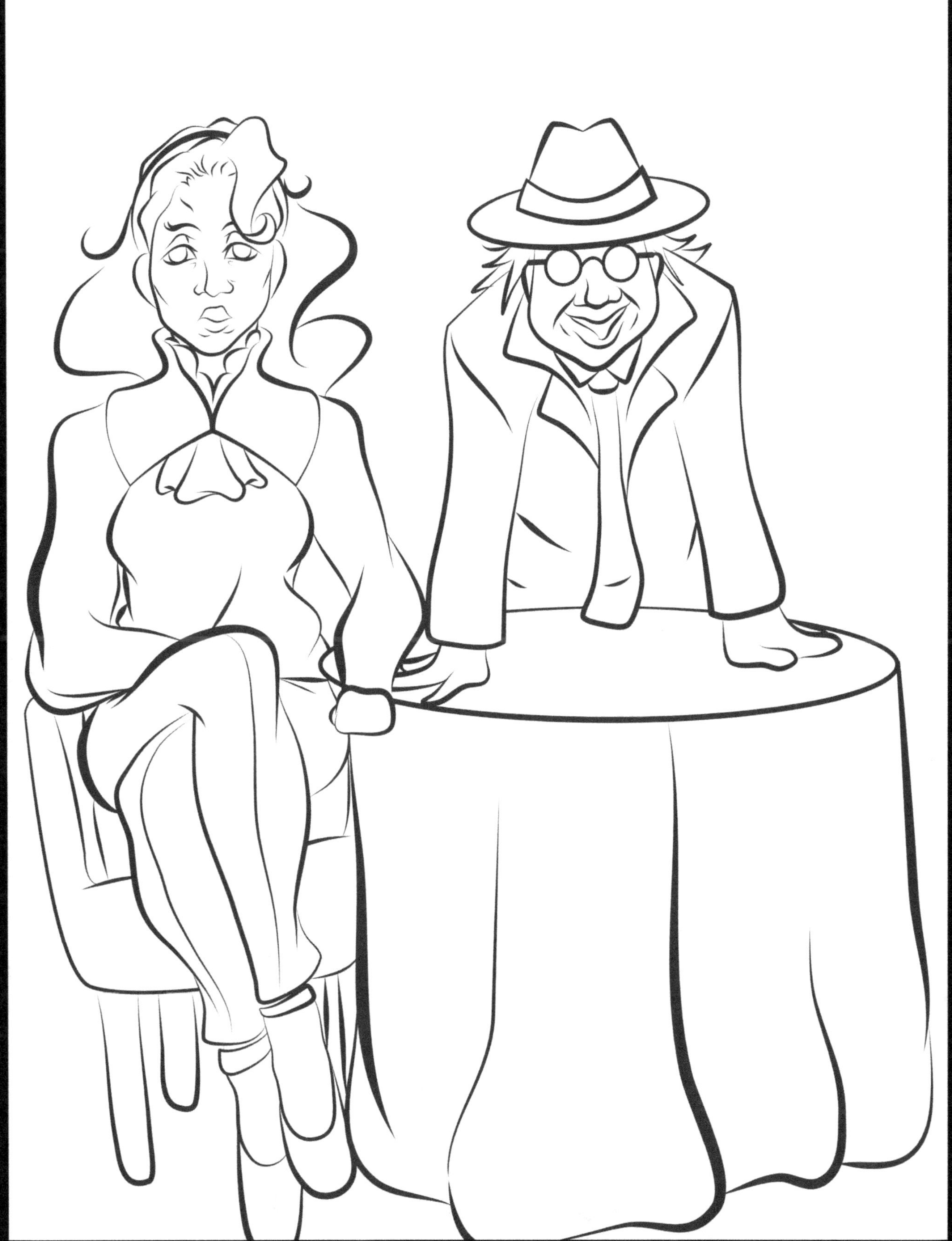

# The Madame and her odd children

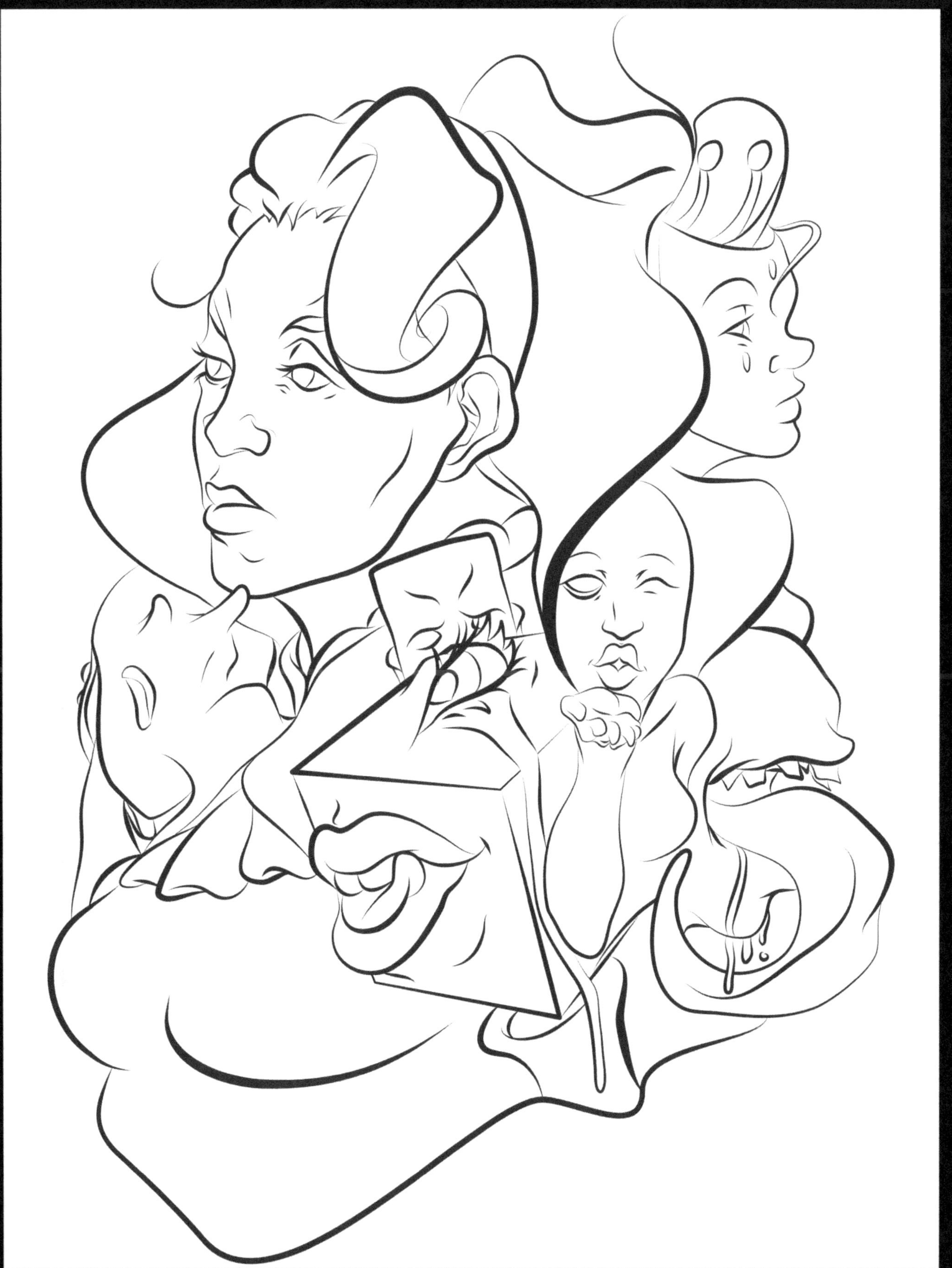

Strike a pose!

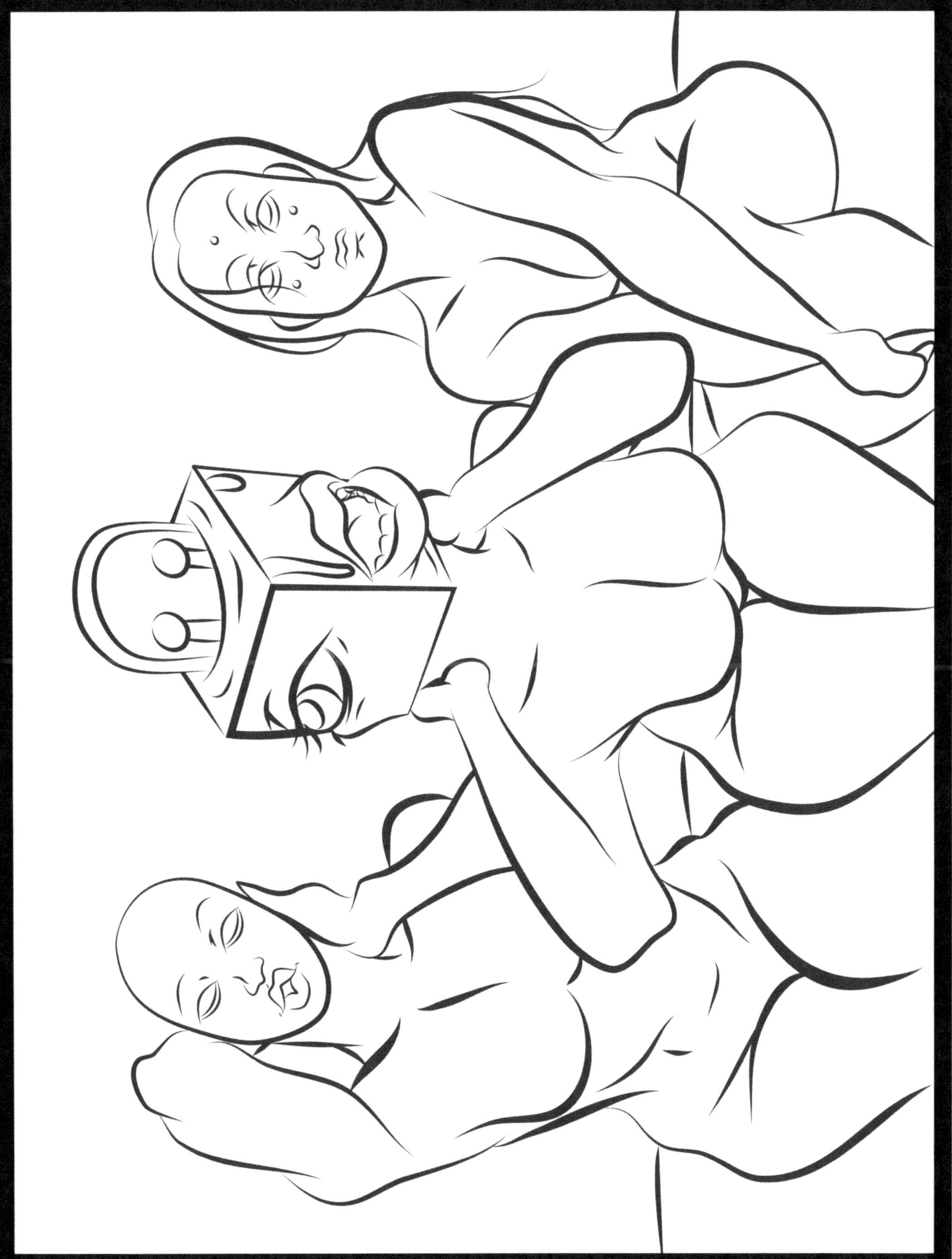

Prepare for battle.

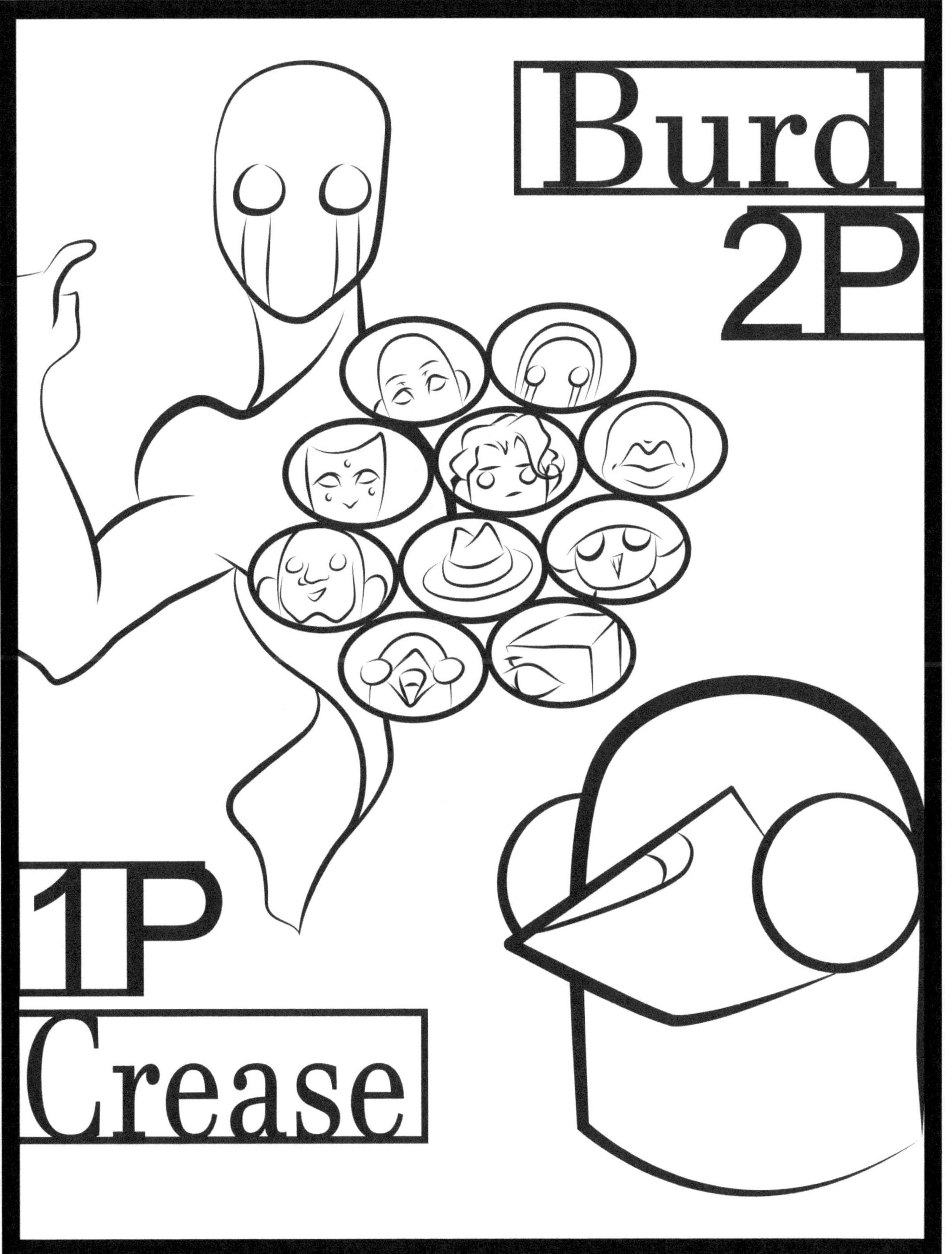
Burd
2P
1P
Crease

Looks like
Crease is
getting pointers
from the pro.

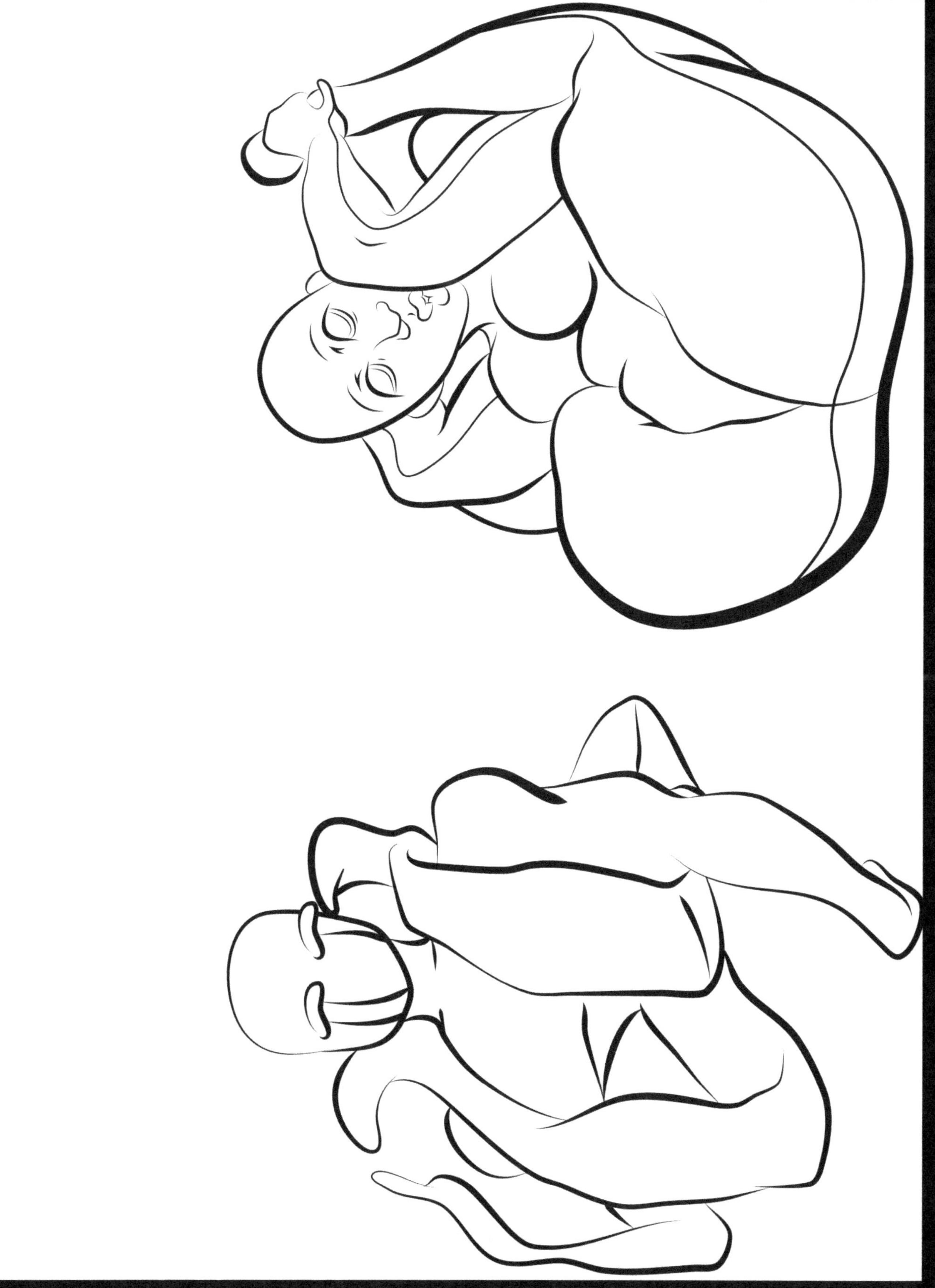

Mesmerizing,
yet frightening.

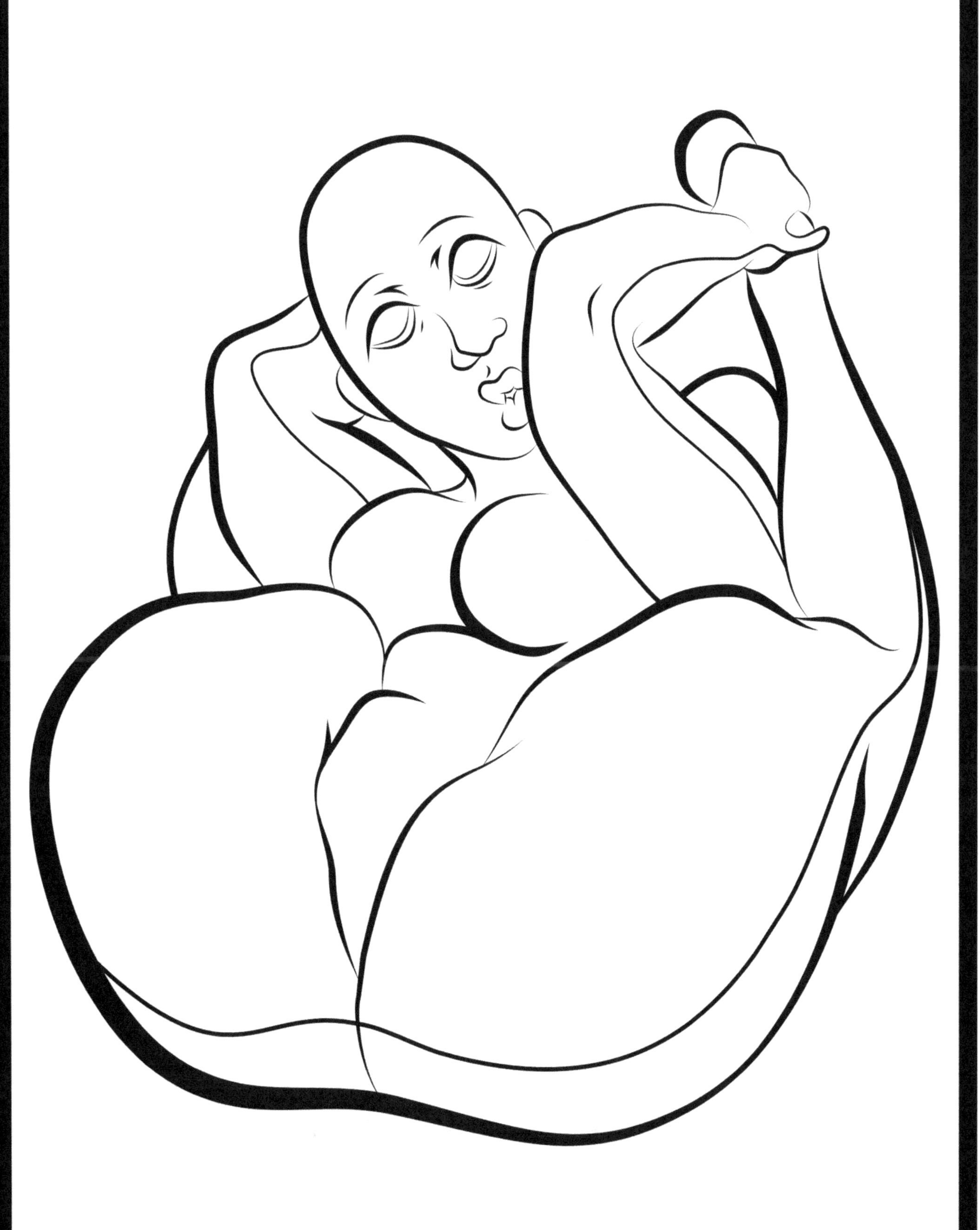

ODD SORT!!!

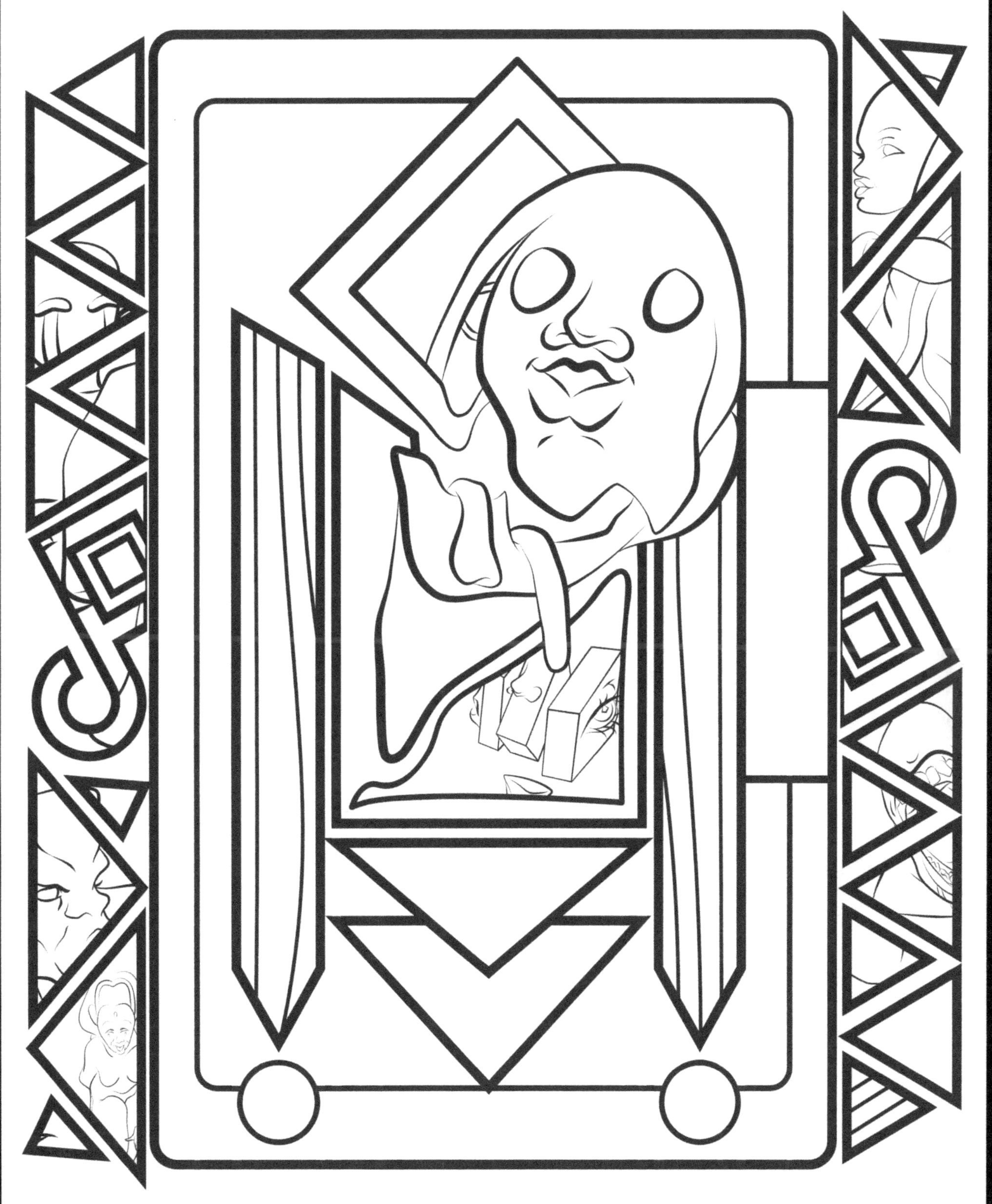

www.ingramcontent.com/pod-product-compliance
Lightning Source LLC
LaVergne TN
LVHW080458160826
845677LV00006B/1402

* 9 7 9 8 4 7 2 2 1 3 9 2 9 *